The Promise and Pain of Loneliness

Michael Angelo Angelo

THE
PROMISE AND PAIN OF
LONELINESS

Steven S. Ivy

BROADMAN PRESS
Nashville, Tennessee

ISBN: 0-8054-5442-X
Dewey Decimal Classification: 152.4
Subject Heading: Loneliness
Library of Congress Catalog Number: 88-7446
Printed in the United States of America

Unless otherwise stated, all Scripture quotations are from the Revised Standard
Version of the Bible, copyrighted 1946, 1952, © 1971, 1973.

Ivy, Stephen S., 1952–
    The Promise and pain of loneliness.

    (The Bible and personal crisis)
    1. Loneliness—Religious aspects—Christianity.
I. Title   II. Series.
BV4911.I89   1989   248.8′6   88-7446
ISBN 0-8054-5442-X

To
Robert and Nancy Ivy,
my father and mother

Who loved me and kept loneliness as far from my heart as was in their power;

Who nurtured me to love others, to be curious, and to risk using God's gifts on behalf of others;

Who taught me to love Scripture and to be faithful on our pilgrimage to the Celestial City.

Contents

1

Loneliness:
Everyone Knows What That Is

"Loneliness!" The word strikes pain and fear into our hearts. The word brings too many unpleasant memories. We remember the time in high school when "all" our friends had Saturday night plans, but not us. We remember the first Christmas apart from a parent or spouse. We imagine the isolation of a homebound friend. We feel the pain of a child not accepted by his classmates. We struggle with the distance caused by physical problems: overweight, addiction, or hospitalization. We avoid the overwhelming pain of separation in death. We struggle with spouses when our busy lives carry us too far into different worlds. Our memories quickly bring to us the pain of loneliness. To read and think about loneliness takes courage.

But we also know that being alone is not the same as being lonely. We remember the creative-writing project which grew out of the Saturday night without plans. We remember the warmth which fills our memories of our deceased parent. We remember the quiet prayer retreat in which no words were spoken, but we felt closer to God and friends than ever before. Loneliness has a positive face as well.

"Then the Lord God said, 'It is not good that the man should be alone; I will make him a helper fit for him'" (Gen. 2:18). Scripture teaches we are created for relationship. Jesus called His disciples to form a community, not to live in isolated discipleship. "This is my commandment, that you love one another as I have loved you" (John

15:12). Yet God's leaders have often sought times of solitude for prayer and discernment. Moses went up the mountain alone and received God's revelation. The prophets frequently were without companions and friends. Jesus took time to seek out lonely places for prayer. We are created for relationships, yet we sometimes grow in times of aloneness. Scripture teaches us that loneliness has both positive and negative potentials.

Is a book on loneliness for you? It is if you struggle at times with the pain that loneliness can bring. Four "typical statements" may help you identify your loneliness. The more of these you can answer with "frequently" or "sometimes," the more likely you are to suffer from loneliness.[1]

1. I never feel in tune with the people around me.
2. I often feel no one really knows me well.
3. I can never find companionship when I want it.
4. I often feel that people are around me but not with me.

This book is also for you if you have a loved one or a friend who struggles with loneliness. Finally, it is for you if you want to know more about how growth can come out of this painful, basic human experience.

This book invites you to journey in the tension of both the pain and promise of loneliness. I will describe the ways in which loneliness is experienced in life. I will also bring scriptural insights to address the pain we sometimes feel. I will attend to the pain and promises of loneliness, so they can instruct us in more creative ways to cope with the pain and to claim the promises.

The Many Faces of Loneliness

T. S. Eliot in "The Elder Statesman" wrote "Oh, loneliness— Everyone knows what that's like." We all do know what loneliness is like. However, we experience loneliness in many different ways. Two persons may each be lonely, yet give very different descriptions of their loneliness. Loneliness comes with many faces. Imagine the faces which go with the following statements.

"I feel that I am not part of any group. No one ever includes me in their activities. I guess I am just different from other people. I just do not fit in with others. Perhaps I do not know how to make friends."

Other faces go with these words: "I am so sad and unhappy. I just feel worthless and inadequate."

Still other faces say: "I just have too much work to do to take time to make friends. I do not like being around other people because I have to see so many people at work every day. I suppose I am just too quiet and thoughtful for others to know I even exist."

The first group of faces represent those who experience loneliness as not having enough social relationships. The second group represents those who experience loneliness as very unpleasant and distressing emotional feelings. The third group summarizes the inner, subjective experience of loneliness. When these three elements combine, a deep and painful condition of loneliness is experienced. One person has defined the experience as "the feeling of not being meaningfully related. It involves the deep hurt of isolation and separation."[2] The hurt of feeling desperate, helpless, unhappy, and separated is painful indeed.

A Closer Look at the Pain

We know the faces of loneliness by recalling lonely experiences in our own lives. But we also know loneliness by the reports of others. Let us allow others' experiences of loneliness to deepen our awareness of this pain.

Robert Frost's "The Road Not Taken" expresses the face of loneliness known by personal decision. You may remember that the poem begins with "Two roads diverged in a yellow wood." The traveler recognizes that two roads lie ahead, and both cannot be traveled.

There is a sense of heaviness and resignation as the traveler decides to travel one path with full knowledge that his decision will make a tremendous difference in his life journey. The heaviness and resignation you may recognize as a kind of loneliness. All of us have made life-changing decisions which have great import. Those decisions are lonely, even when we have family and friends to share in the decision-making process.

We feel another kind of loneliness when we do not have a supportive community. For example, Psalm 31:9-11 expresses the face of loneliness when our community turns away:

> Be gracious to me, O Lord, for I am in distress;
>   my eye is wasted from grief,
>   my soul and my body also.
> For my life is spent with sorrow,
>   and my years with sighing;
> My strength fails because of my misery,
>   and my bones waste away.
>
> I am the scorn of my adversaries,
>   a horror to my neighbors,
> an object of dread to my acquaintances;
>   those who see me in the street flee from me.

This face of loneliness is well known when we suffer and friends and family do not understand our hopes and dreams. It is familiar to those of us who are rejected because of different ideas, different physical appearances, and different life-styles.

We can see other faces of loneliness in grief following the death of loved ones. When close ties of love and companionship are severed, we are cut adrift. There are feelings of being abandoned. Deep and fearful emotions grow within the grieving heart. Anger, sadness, and fear may overwhelm and block out all good relationships. John Claypool in *Tracks of a Fellow Struggler* recorded his experiences of grief and community during the illness and death of his daughter. The face of loneliness he pictured was informed by God's gifts to him. Yet the core loneliness of walking that path was clear. He found his loss to be a deep shock. It included questions such as: "Where do I go from here? Is there a road out, and if so, which one?"[3] Yet his grief was also a gift.

> The way of remorse does not alter the stark reality [of death] one whit and only makes matters worse. The way of gratitude does not alleviate the pain, but it somehow puts some light around the darkness and builds strength to begin to move on.[4]

Many lonely persons in grief are more likely to focus on the questions and pain. Most find it more difficult to affirm their gratitude for the strength which is given.

Another face of loneliness is seen in depression. Depression is an emotional illness in which the sufferer feels helpless and hopeless. A record producer recently wrote of a time in his life when he was being very successful in his job. He was producing hit gospel recordings. Yet his inner world was in great turmoil. He felt out of control and had no idea which way to turn. The symptoms he described were those of anxiety depression. He wrote that he began conquering his depression when he was able to pray, "Lord, forgive me, . . . Teach me to submit myself to You. You are bigger than my problem. I will quit making demands; I trust you."[5] The key to his prayer was his willingness to trust, to enter a relationship. This was a step out of his loneliness and into relationship.

Sometimes loneliness wears the face of physical illness. Several medical studies have reported that those who live alone and isolated lives are more likely to suffer from a variety of chronic and severe diseases. Dr. James Lynch in *The Broken Heart* reported that early death is closely related to one's relationships. He wrote that death rates are consistently higher for the divorced, widowed, and never married than for married persons. For example, married smokers have about the same death rate as divorced nonsmokers. Further, Lynch found that when a person is abandoned by one or both parents at an early age, he is more likely to die at a younger adult age. In general, Dr. Lynch found that positive human relationships help prevent serious illnesses and premature death. Other studies have shown that lonely persons are more likely to have physical complaints and go to doctors more frequently than the nonlonely.[6] Further, hospitalized patients who have little family support and few visitors are more likely to give up on their treatments and die than those who have family and friends to support and encourage them.[7] In general, loneliness creates and increases stress. Stress is unhealthy. Relationships are crucial to good health.

Another face of loneliness is seen in the ways in which close relationships are missed.[8] Some lonely persons are very dissatisfied with their relationships. They have no intimate relationships. Even attachments to neighbors are of little significance. Frequently these persons blame others for their loneliness. They feel as if they are not important to anyone, as if they have "been placed on a shelf and forgotten." Other lonely persons have social contacts through church, school, community, and work organizations. However, they lack a deep, intimate attachment. They believe, however, that their loneliness is only temporary. Divorced persons often experience this type of loneliness. They may have lonely feelings, but they can fill their time with social activities and expect that the feelings will go away. A third group of lonely persons have few friends but are not dissatisfied with their situation. They do not blame others but seem resigned and hopeless in response to their loneliness. Many widowed women represent this type of loneliness. Feelings of boredom and uselessness seem to dominate.

Of course, there are many other faces to loneliness. I will examine these in the chapters which follow. At this point, I simply want to help you begin to identify the fact that loneliness is not the same experience in all people. Loneliness comes in many different forms. Which of these faces most clearly resembles your loneliness?

Keys to Recognizing Lonely Faces

The faces of loneliness can be remembered through three key ingredients. First, lonely persons have an awareness that something is missing. They feel an absence or an emptiness that is uncomfortable. External conditions such as grief, failure, and life changes may bring on this feeling. Second, lonely persons are searching. Until persons begin to struggle for relationship they are not lonely although they may be alone. Third, when persons become aware of their loneliness, they are faced with an internal choice of how to proceed. At this point, the face of loneliness becomes one of responsibility.[9] Lonely persons become accountable for their choices. Awareness, search, and accountability are the hallmarks of loneliness.

Several elements of the experience of loneliness are clear. First, loneliness involves the inner perceptions, reactions, and emotions which have negative meanings. Second, loneliness involves a separation from loved ones or a perceived lack of relationships. Third, loneliness is an experience which is shared by all persons.

These faces will be more fully and carefully examined in this book. My intention is to help those who are lonely decrease their fear and isolation. I also hope that the coping strategies will enable you who are lonely to more effectively transform loneliness into community and solitude. My prayer is that those who are lonely and those who care for them will be strengthened through reading this book.

Loneliness in Biblical and Human Perspective

Persons are created for relationship with others, with creation, and with God. Yet loneliness is both a human problem and part of the human condition. The faces of loneliness tell us how persons are separated from others by isolation, trauma, and grief. The faces of loneliness tell us how persons are separated from creation by inattention and depression. The faces of loneliness tell us how persons feel separated from God, from any sense of life purpose and meaning. In what way is there a convergence between the biblical understanding of persons and the concrete experiences of lonely people? How are we to understand and respond to the pain and promise of loneliness? This book will respond to these questions. However, a general perspective on the problem can be identified already.

First, loneliness is both painful and promising. It is painful to know how different I am from others. The prophet Elijah was sure he was all alone in his dedication to God's cause. He isolated himself and hid in a cave because of his conviction (1 Kings 19). It is painful to feel isolated, self-hatred, and meaninglessness. King David feared for his kingdom and life when his sin with Bathsheba so clearly confronted him (2 Sam. 11).

But there is also promise. Abraham's willingness to leave his familiar home led him into many lonely circumstances, yet his faith formed the basis of God's covenant with the people of Israel. Jesus frequently sought out "lonely places" for prayer and meditation. Loneliness may be turned to solitude when it is dedicated to a cause, a project, or God. When loneliness turns to solitude, its promise is fully experienced.

Second, loneliness is a universal experience. No person needs to feel ashamed or unusual because of feeling lonely. All of us experience loneliness at times. Two reasons are already clear for this. God created us as individuals. We sin as individuals. A part of the human condition is that we can never be perfectly in tune with another person. While we are more alike than we are different, each of us is created unique. All experience this kind of loneliness which is sometimes seen in inner feelings of separation from others and God. A part of the human problem is that we make wrong choices: we hurt others and self, we destroy God's creation, and we do not fully live our lives in accord with God. All experience this kind of loneliness which is seen in situations such as broken marriages, tragic conflicts, and unhealthy parenting.

Third, loneliness comes in many guises. The "faces of loneliness" remind us not to be too quick to offer simple solutions to a very complex human experience. Thus, I will examine our experiences of loneliness through a variety of settings. In chapter 2, I will explore the loneliness which is natural to the human life process. There are familiar experiences of "not having anyone to play with," of "not having a date for the prom," of losing a sense of one's life direction during the "mid-life crisis," and of adjusting to the death of one's spouse. The promise of growth and change offers ways of coping with this loneliness.

In chapter 3, I will explore the loneliness which is characterized by emotional distress. These experiences are rooted in such emotional experiences as grief and depression. The promise of emotional nurture offers comfort.

In chapter 4, I will discuss the loneliness experienced as the pain of social isolation. These experiences often result from broken relationships such as pained marriages and substance abuse. The promise of community offers hope.

In chapter 5, I will examine the pain of loneliness which results from separation from God. The promise of solitude offers conversion into the presence of God.

The final chapter will focus on caring for those who are lonely. This chapter will shift in emphasis from those who are lonely to those who offer love and support to the lonely. How can others enable the lonely to claim the promises of loneliness?

This outline should indicate that I know loneliness is a concern for every person. It should also be clear that I believe that our loneliness must be carefully examined in order to respond in creative and freeing ways. Thus, the coping strategies and suggestions for change which will be found in this book are meant to be carefully considered by you, the reader. You may identify closely with some descriptions of loneliness because they are your own. Other descriptions will not match your experience. Similarly, some of my suggestions for responding to loneliness will fit you, and others will not. I must trust you to carefully consider your own experience as I lead you through understanding loneliness.

I invite you to join me on this courageous adventure through the paths of loneliness. We will meet much pain. But we will also meet tremendous promise.

A Biblical Perspective

Why do persons feel lonely? What can be done to cope with that loneliness? The promise and pain of loneliness are well described in the biblical record. These descriptions begin with the creation accounts, carry through the Old Testament stories of God's covenant people, climax with the redeeming love of Jesus Christ, and conclude with the relationships of God's New Covenant community: the church. Scripture tells us of persons who were separated from ones they loved. Ruth, Job, David, Jeremiah, and Hosea are but a few of those who suffered broken relationships and the accompanying pangs of loneliness. We know of others who suffered a spiritual loneliness in which they were separated from a sense of life's meaning and purpose. Perhaps the rich young ruler and Saul of Tarsus best characterized this sense of separation from what is most meaningful. By reflecting upon these persons, we can come to understand the core nature of persons. Our nature leads to both the loneliness of separation from loving relationships and of separation from our Creator.

The Creation Story

Scripture begins with the affirmation that persons were created for relationship with God and each other (Gen. 1:27; 2:18). Men and women are social by nature. We were created to live in partnership with each other and with God. The story of Adam and Eve indicates they were partners in relationship to each other, creation, and their Creator. We are also told that they were created in the "image of God" (Gen. 1:27). I believe that their need for relationship is a key meaning of being created in "the image of God." Certainly this scriptural affirmation has been understood in many ways. However, one meaning is that persons are like God in their capacity for relational and creative love. As Paul wrote, "None of us lives to himself, and none of us dies to himself" (Rom. 14:7). In life and in death, we long for human community.

Yet Scripture also affirms that we are created as individuals with unique identities and futures. We are separated from other people. We can never feel exactly what another feels, never completely understand another's thoughts, and never do anything exactly like another person. An artist's work is recognizable by a unique use of the brush and color, even when the artist is attempting to faithfully copy the work of another. So our lives are unique to us as individuals. We stand as strangers before each other and separated from God. Thus, we are caught in the tension between individuality and community, between solitude and solidarity.[10] Our past histories are unique, and our future directions are unique. Yet Scripture affirms that God will bring all our individual stories to completion within God's purposes. All our uniqueness will find fulfillment within God's plan.

The creation accounts also record that persons seldom discover the proper balance between living alone and in community. The perfect community of Adam and Eve with each other, creation, and God was broken in their first sin. The biblical creation accounts clearly tie experiences of guilt, shame, pain, and death to separation from God. That is, our loneliness is not simply separation from other persons. The essence of our loneliness is separation from God. The good news is that Jesus' radical trust in God offer new hope for healing our bro-kenness and loneliness. Because He trusted God fully and died on our behalf, we do not have to bear fully the anguish of separation from God.

Is loneliness then a result of the fall? In my judgment, it is primar-ily a part of the suffering which results from our being part of crea-tion. Adam and Eve had physical limits and thus experienced finitude prior to their sin. They had moral limits and thus experienced tempta-tion prior to their sin. They were separate individuals and thus experi-enced loneliness prior to their sin. These experiences were of a different character than the results of their sin which included illness, cruelty, and death. Isolation and vulnerability are inescapable ele-ments of the human condition. Loneliness is part of the fact of being human for which God gave us community. It is a burden which de-mands community.

The Old Testament Witness

The biblical story moves from creation through a series of individ-ual and family histories. These histories culminate in the story of the people of God's covenant, the Jews. These stories include within them elements of individual striving and community relationships. They include positive experiences of relationships with others and God. They also include stories of loneliness and sin. The Old Testa-ment is full of accounts in which persons are torn by their promises and friendships. Stories about families and friendships are thus the ways in which we learn about persons and God in the Old Testament.

The accounts of the prophets contrast with the accounts of the his-torians. Both focus on the communication between individuals and their communities. Yet the prophets condemned both rugged individ-ualism and absorption into a group. We too experience the pain of either living alone or losing our identity in the group. We struggle to live in ways which both deny self and affirm self. Jesus said, "If any man would come after me, let him deny himself and take up his cross and follow me" (Mark 8:34). He also said, "You shall love your neighbor *as yourself*" (Mark 12:31, author's italics). We tend to land on one side or the other. Rugged individualists try to be complete within themselves. Others give up self to depend upon others. Each stance is an example of sin at work in individuals and relationships. Each results in loneliness.

At the very core of our lives there are serious questions which may move us to loneliness. "Who am I?" reveals our striving for identity. "Whom can I trust?" reveals our striving for community. "Where do I fit?" reveals our striving for vocation. How we answer these questions determines the balance of individuality and community in our lives. Our answers to these questions also place us in the tension of the promise and pain of loneliness. We are born as separate selves. Yet we live our lives in search for affirmation and love. "Only a loved life is a life that can be experienced as human."[11] Thus, "woe to him who is alone" (Eccl. 4:10) echoes our deep need for companionship. The people of the Old Testament asked these questions and lived their answers in a variety of ways. Their answers produced both community and loneliness throughout Israel's history.

The Difference Jesus Made

God's people were not able to create the balance of self and community necessary for living fully in balance with others, creation, and God. Indeed, their loneliness was manifested by their pain related to both death and guilt. Their human need for rootedness and identity was not met by either the religious or political communities of their day. Jesus Christ was born into this struggle. God's relationship to His people was restored in Jesus. While Jesus was often alone, we are never told that He was lonely. He related to created nature with power and sensitivity. His relationship to His Father in heaven was perfect. In Christ we see God's answer to our natural condition of separation and our sinful condition of fear and guilt. Jesus calls for a response. Through a faithful relationship with Him we may find deeper springs of relationship than we had ever dreamed possible. We thus live creatively by expressing our love through faith and commitment to Jesus Christ.

Yet the biblical story does not end here. It continues with the formation of people who share their joys and sufferings in powerful ways. In their companionship there emerged purpose and work which provided clear vocation for their lives. They were able to share meaningful prayer, to touch others with healing, and to change their lives from being slaves to being free under God. But their loneliness was never totally healed. They still fought, disagreed, and felt separated from each other. Yet it was clear that in the formation of the church, God was at work for peace. Here was proclaimed that "in Christ God was reconciling the world to himself, not counting their trespasses against them, and entrusting to us the message of reconciliation" (2 Cor. 5:19). The vocation of those who call themselves Christian is thus to be reconcilers. Reconcilers bring together those who are separated and broken in life. The church is called to be God's agent to create community and healing in this world. The church knows both the pain and promise of loneliness.

Even though our deepest loneliness belongs to our human condition, we must see it as a human problem as well. Our ultimate loneliness is ministered to only by faith in Jesus Christ. Our experiences of human loneliness may have different avenues of healing.

Notes

1. Daniel Russell, "The Measurement of Loneliness," *Loneliness: A Sourcebook of Current Theory, Research, and Therapy,* eds. Letitia A. Peplau and Daniel Perlman (New York: Wiley and Sons, 1982), p. 94.

2. Harvey H. Potthoff, *Loneliness: Understanding and Dealing with It* (Nashville: Abingdon Press, 1976), p. 11.

3. John Claypool, *Tracks of a Fellow Struggler* (Waco, Texas: Word Books, 1974), p. 71.

4. Claypool, p. 83.

5. Michael Omartian, "Who's in Charge?" *Guideposts,* Sept. 1987, p. 37.

6. Vira R. Kivett, "Discriminators of Loneliness Among the Rural Elderly," *The Gerontologist,* 19 (1979), pp. 107-115. Stig Berg, and others, "Loneliness in the Swedish Elderly," *Journal of Geronotology,* 36 (1981), pp. 342-349.

7. Randall Stout, "Coping with Loneliness," *Bulletin of the College of Chaplains,* 1983, pp. 84-90.

8. Jenny de Jong-Gierveld and Jos Raadschelders, "Types of Loneliness," *Loneliness: A Sourcebook,* pp. 114-117.

9. Robert Neale, "Loneliness, Depression, Grief, and Alienation," *Clinical Handbook of Pastoral Counseling,* eds. Robert Wicks, R. Parsons, and D. Capps, (New York: Paulist Press, 1985), pp. 466-467.

10. Frank Stagg, *Polarities of Man's Existence in Biblical Perspective* (Philadelphia: Westminster Press, 1973), pp. 75-76.

11. Jürgen Moltmann, *God in Creation* (New York: Harper and Row, 1985), p. 268.

2

Loneliness and the Seasons of Life

"For everything there is a season, and a time for every matter under heaven" (Eccl. 3:1). We know this truth in the experiences of our inner lives, our relationships with persons, and our relationship with God. Life is a matter of seasons. Behaviors, thoughts, and feelings which are expected at one time in life are totally out of place at another time. We can expect both the two-year-old and the twenty-two-year-old to become frustrated and angry when others will not do what they want. The frustrated two-year-old may lie down on the floor, scream, and kick his feet. We recognize his behavior as a "temper tantrum." Such displays are expected and should be of little concern to parents and other caretakers, at least as long as they remain within certain boundaries. However, if the twenty-two-year-old responds with a similar outburst, those who care for the man should be very concerned. He does need help with his self-expression.

Some experiences of loneliness are related to the seasons of life. Two-year-old, twenty-two-year-old, and seventy-two-year-old persons will each feel loneliness. However, they will feel loneliness in very different ways and from different causes. Their loneliness will therefore require different responses. The writer of Ecclesiastes was well aware of the difference that age makes in one's needs and attitudes.

For if a man lives many years, let him rejoice in them all; but let him remember that the days of darkness will be many. All that comes in vanity.

Rejoice, O young man, in your youth, and let your heart cheer you in the days of your youth; walk in the ways of your heart and the sight of your eyes. But know that for all these things God will bring you into judgment (Eccl. 11:8-9).

It is important to understand the nature of the developing person in order to respond to the pain and promise of loneliness through one's life.

This chapter will examine the ways in which these life cycle changes bring unique experiences of loneliness. We know that the experiences which cause a five-year-old to feel "lonely" are not the same for those who are fifteen, thirty-five, fifty-five, or seventy-five years old. The loneliness of the five-year-old who finds kindergarten difficult is very different from the loneliness of the ill seventy-five-year-old who will never be able to return home again. Both Scripture and studies in human development can help us understand the experiences of loneliness which are unique to each season of life.

Human Development in Scriptural Perspective

"For everything there is a season" is a biblical principle which is also found in the common wisdom of our culture. Most people seem to agree with the notion that time brings changes. Time and change are deeply rooted in our awareness. We seem to naturally think of life having at least three seasons. First there is the experience of getting started in life that lasts approximately twenty years. Then there is the adult period which lasts until perhaps age sixty-five. The final period is the ending phase from age sixty-five to death. Youth, adulthood, and old age are clearly discernable seasons of life.

In order to fully understand the nature of loneliness which results from the natural changes in our lives, we need to think further about our experiences of community. Scripture clearly tells us of the interdependence of all creation. Humans are given "dominion over" every creature and are given everything they need for food (Gen. 1:28-29). Thus, when sin entered human life, all creation suffered as well. "Cursed is the ground because of you" (Gen. 3:17). As part of God's creation, we are related to every other part. The Genesis accounts also tell us of the purposefulness of creation. All aspects of creation share in God's ultimate purpose that all be transformed into the perfect creation of God (Rom. 8:19-24). The relationships of creation are an essential element in the development of persons.

Similarly, every part of life's journey from infancy through old age depends upon God's gracious care. Indeed, it is only God's holiness which gives a basis for the hope which sustains us, whether through loneliness or through friendship. Our purpose as children of God depends upon the wonderful ways in which God cares for us and directs our life journey.

"For everything there is a season" states the theme for the current balance of creation. God is certainly sovereign in all matters of time and development. However, there is a kind of balance and repetitiveness according to "the Preacher" of Ecclesiastes. This is most clearly seen in Ecclesiastes 3:1-8:

> For everything there is a season, and a time for every
>   matter under heaven:
> a time to be born, and a time to die;
> a time to plant, and a time to pluck up what is planted;
> a time to kill, and a time to heal;
> a time to break down, and a time to build up;
> a time to weep, and a time to laugh;
> a time to mourn, and a time to dance;
> a time to cast away stones, and a time to gather
>   stones together;

a time to embrace, and a time to refrain from
    embracing;
a time to seek, and a time to lose;
a time to keep, and a time to cast away;
a time to rend, and a time to sew;
a time to keep silence, and a time to speak;
a time to love, and a time to hate;
a time for war, and a time for peace.
What gain has the worker from his toil?

The "Preacher" wrote about the tensions of life within which we live. Life and death, killing and healing, mourning, and dancing each have their place within each person's developmental life history. These changes are certainly perplexing. But change does provide the background against which God's purposes are worked out.

The occurrences ("times") of life mark life's movement and direction. The seasons of life are somewhat fixed and determined. Hence, God has appointed the processes of life. Our developmental histories place us in the progression of events which are not within our control. Loneliness is but one of the many tensions of life. Loneliness and community, solitude and company, aloneness and companionship are some of the dynamic experiences through which we shape our lives.

However, the Preacher's sense of futility within this time-bound perspective was not the final story. The worker's toil is not in vain! In Ephesians Paul wrote about the need of "Redeeming the time" (Eph. 5:16, KJV). The redemptive work of Christ on our behalf extends to the nature of time itself. While the repetitive cycles of life may create one life boundary, they do not bind us. In Christ we are free to transcend these limits. Ecclesiastes 3:1-8 should guide us to patient courage rather than rigid fatalism.

The Preacher is calling us to the importance of timing in all our life activities. When a golfer swings his club, the force of the swing is not very important. What is really important is the timing with which he swings. The musician knows that playing the right time and rhythm for the music is as important as playing the right notes. The gardener respects the seasons and only plants seeds when the time is right. Similarly, when it is time to grieve, newness of life can be discovered in that grieving. When it is time to remember God's gracious actions on behalf of our salvation, new life begins to form deep inside. When the season of life calls for aloneness, perhaps even loneliness, patient acceptance and courage can be nurtured. Experiences of loneliness are frequently shaped by the time of life in which events occur. Development helps focus our attention on the importance of good timing.[1]

The Seasons of Individual Development

"For everything there is a season" is a biblical principle which corresponds to knowledge from studies in human development. The idea that persons change and develop throughout life is the special focus of "life-span development studies." This field studies the needs and expectations of persons at different times in their life journey. While there are many different theories of development, all agree that persons have patterns of change and development throughout life.

Life-span development studies do not agree on the number of stages of life. They have named between three and fifteen seasons. They do not agree on the best focus for their studies. They have focused on biological development, religious development, career development, moral development, personality development, and a host of others. Perhaps scientific studies have made the human life journey seem much more complex than it really is. But they do serve the purpose of helping us understand the marvelous ways in which God has created us to grow in relation to self, neighbor, and God.

There are at least three principles generally accepted by life-span development researchers. Each of these principles emphasizes the process of growth and change. I believe that these principles are harmonious with scriptural understandings of persons as well.

(1) Change involves the entire person. (2) Growth changes relation-ships. (3) Persons are always changing. These principles are both biblically and developmentally true. They will help us understand the natural experiences of loneliness throughout the life span.

Change Is Wholistic

Change involves the entire person. Jesus told us to "love the Lord your God with all your heart, and with all your soul, and with all your strength, and with all your mind; and your neighbor as yourself" (Luke 10:27). The key aspects of self are emotion, spirit, body, intel-lect, and relationship. Developmental psychologies study each of these aspects of personhood, although few study all in a balanced perspective. Most emphasize one aspect out of proportion to the others. Nevertheless, they agree that each of these elements of personhood changes. Change never leaves us the same. For example, the child whose body begins to grow into maturity is also expected to mature in intellect. The middle adult whose relationships are changed by death or by geographic moves is also expected to mature spiritu-ally.

Change in any aspect of life sometimes results in loneliness. Those who have moved away from friends and family for school or job cer-tainly know how geographic moves may bring loneliness. It may not be quite so obvious how a growth in emotional maturity may bring loneliness. Think for a moment of the girl who is a senior in high school. Her friends are most interested in being similar to each other, being with the "in crowd." However, her emotional growth may lead her to focus more on her personal interests, to be more concerned for her own values than for the values of her group. She is moving into the young adult level of maturity. This may be a lonely period because she feels different. Indeed she may have few social relationships which support her new sense of self-direction. We change in all aspects of self throughout life. These changes will frequently leave us feeling lonely for some period of time.

Change Is Relational

A second principle is that growth changes relationships. Our life is lived through a balance of relationships. These changes can be understood as "self-other balances."[2] Self-other balances point to the different ways in which we live in relationships. For example, the total dependency of the infant on her mother is very different from her adolescent moves for independence. That is, relationships between myself and others are forever changing in their texture and balance. The balance of self-other relational needs change throughout life.

The biblical story of Joseph illustrates this principle well (see Gen. 37; 39—47; 50). Joseph was his father's (Jacob) favorite son. His older brothers were jealous but could not touch him as long as he stayed at home. That protection changed when he became old enough to join them in the fields. This developmental change meant that they could attack him and sell him into slavery. His entrance into young adulthood meant that he was no longer under the protection of this father. Later, through the providence of God, Jacob's relationships with his father and brothers again changed. As adults they became dependent upon him because he had prospered under a foreign power. There was a subtle balance between self and other at every season in their life journey.

What do these changes in self-other relationships look like? We know that needs for independence and inclusion are always in tension and always changing. Independence refers to the human need for self-direction, for making our own decisions, for feeling autonomous from others. Inclusion refers to our need to stay related to others, to be attached to communities and individuals. For example, the adolescent strives for independence from parents. Sometimes that striving takes on rather outlandish expressions in clothing and music. At the same time, however, the adolescent has powerful needs to be included in a peer group, to be attached to those like him.

In contrast, think for a moment about the elderly adult. During this season of life independence and autonomy becomes increasingly difficult and burdensome. The task of the elderly adult is to accept these changes as they occur and experience ways of being more dependent on, more attached to, others.

This way of understanding the seasons of life emphasizes the importance both of individual direction and of community at every life stage. We are never without need for community. We are never without need for individuality. The ways in which we need community change. These changes can sometimes lead to experiences of loneliness.

Change Is Constant

Life is always in process. This principle emphasizes that change is always happening. But, the motion of these changes has a pattern which is constant for all persons. This pattern is called the "developmental stages." We have learned to think about the stages of infancy, childhood, adolescence, young adulthood, middle adulthood, and older adulthood. It is very interesting to describe the distinguishing signs—physical, emotional, and spiritual—for each era.

However, it is most interesting to think about the powerful changes which occur between eras of life. The changes which happen between adolescence and young adulthood are more fascinating than the features of either stage taken alone. For every gain that a new season of life offers, there is certainly also a loss. The toddler who stops crawling in order to walk risks many bruises and loses some dependence. He gains freedom and a new perspective on the world. Thus, the nature of change is crucial to understanding the human life span.

The human journey involves letting go in order to move forward. But that very letting go is also a kind of death to an old way of living. Jesus said, "Truly, truly, I say to you, unless a grain of wheat falls into the earth and dies, it remains alone; but if it dies, it bears much fruit" (John 12:24). He was certainly referring to His own death and resurrection. But the parable also illustrates the change principle of life. Old, worn-out ways of living must regularly die so that new ways of living can emerge. For example, the way the young adult experiences her world must die, if she is to deal with her world effectively as a middle-aged adult.

There is a price to be paid for this constant life motion. During times of change we may sometimes feel that everything is coming loose at the seams. That is, when the motion of change becomes too fast, and changes are too drastic, we may become disoriented and disillusioned. Loneliness may be experienced during these times of change. The person who has recently retired may feel this burden. His former daily habits change. He is not around his friends at work. He has more time to think and to play. He has more opportunity to be with spouse and neighbors. He can volunteer more of his time for church projects. But he also may have lost some measure of respect and self-esteem because he is "getting old." Each of these changes has both positive and negative aspects. There is something gained and something lost emotionally and spiritually during all times of change.

The Seasons of Relational Development

Loneliness involves our relationships with self, others, and God. It is important to more clearly understand the ways in which we relate to each other if we are to see the ways in which loneliness is experienced naturally throughout life. Three aspects of every relationship can be described which will help understand the complexity of loneliness during the seasons of life. In relationships we may let go, hold on, and stay put.[3] The nature of loneliness can be understood by the interaction of these relational motifs.

Letting Go

Development requires seasons of letting go in relationships. Jesus used the image of the seed which must fall into the ground and die if it is to grow as a metaphor for the Christian life. We must die before we can be born. Parents know this pain. In order for the toddler to learn to walk, parents must be willing to let go and allow the child to fall. Later, the school-age child cannot learn to ride a bicycle without suffering through spills and accidents. The teenager will not learn to correctly make important decisions unless opportunity is given to make bad decisions.

As adults we sometimes must say good-bye to friends only to discover that the pain of leaving opens up deeper and richer friendships. Growth in marriage sometimes involves one spouse letting go of the other enough to risk new investments of time and energy. Relationships which are willing to let go are essential for growth to occur.

Holding On

Growth also depends upon relationships which will hold on. We frequently think of God's love as the perfect support. The hymn "God Will Take Care of You" speaks of the love of God which stays with us through all of life's joys and pains.

> Be not dismayed whate'er betide,
> God will take care of you;
> Beneath his wings of love abide,
> God will take care of you.
> . . . .
> No matter what may be the test,
> God will take care of you;

> Lean, weary one, upon his breast,
> God will take care of you.

Of course, God's love includes letting go as we are given responsibility for moral decisions and life-style choices. God's holding on is indeed graceful. Perhaps *grace* is a good word to communicate the balance of relationships.

In human relationships this balance of holding on and letting go can be difficult to achieve. Parents who let go of their children so much that their children feel abandoned and alone are not holding on in healthy ways. This leads to fundamental problems in families. During the times when one season of life is changing to another there may be pain and conflict in the holding on. We know that the change of weather seasons can be very tumultuous. The late spring snowstorm or the fall hurricane are clear examples from nature that when forces are changing, both danger and power are present.

Holding on to persons during times of change requires willingness to love and support even when there is tumult and pain. Holding on to the young adolescent requires setting clear boundaries and expecting her to live within them. It also calls for parents and teachers to be patient when she pushes at the boundaries. Holding on to the forty-year-old man may mean supporting him through difficult vocational changes as his developing self takes a new career direction.

Staying Put

Healthy growth also depends upon relationships which will stay put. For relationships to stay put means that the community which is most important to the changing person is available both during and after the time of change. For example, the preschooler who is entering school is usually growing through a rather dramatic change. His parents are the most important persons to him during this change. A divorce or death at this time can be very traumatic because his key relationships did not stay put. In contrast, the key relationships for adolescents are their friends. A parental divorce during adolescence may be painful to the young person, but if she does not have to leave her friends because of the divorce, the pain will usually not be overly traumatic.

As we think of the nature of relationships through life changes we can readily see that pain is inevitable. There will certainly be times of emotional and spiritual hurt, including the presence of loneliness. No human relationship will perfectly let go, hold on, and stay put throughout life.

We can also recognize that pain is not necessarily bad. Sometimes it cannot be avoided and may provide a deep possibility for growth. A friend told me of one of the loneliest times of his life. It occurred during his senior year of high school. His father was required to take a job in a nearby city, but the family did not move until after his graduation. His father's leaving home for those six months changed his interests in school, sports, and his future. He deeply felt his father's absence during a crucial time in his development. While this was a spiritually painful time, it was also a rich time of growth and development. Indeed, during this time he experienced the initial stirrings of awareness which eventually led to his accepting God's call to ministry. Although his family did not stay put and he felt very lonely, God used the experience for good.

Relationships have differing functions throughout our life cycles. Thus, the human life cycle is marked by a tension between separateness and fulfilling relationships. The psalmist knew the turmoil which marks our lives.

> For all our days pass away under thy wrath.
> our years come to an end like a sigh.
> The years of our life are threescore and ten,
> or even by reason of strength fourscore;

> yet their span is but toil and trouble;
>> they are soon gone, and we fly away.
> So teach us to number our days
>> that we get a heart of wisdom (Ps. 90:9-10,12).

The heart of wisdom is prepared for the dramatic, yet predictable, changes through which our relationships proceed in life. The heart of wisdom allows relationships to blossom, grow, and change according to the life cycle. The heart of wisdom holds on, lets go, and stays put throughout the changes of life.

Loneliness through the Life Cycle

Up to now in this chapter I have been discussing a general understanding of human development. I have discussed the importance of relationships, some expected changes in relationships, and some key elements in those changes. Now I will consider more directly some of the expected loneliness at specific times during the seasons of life.

Certainly change, growth, and development are the essence of life. Relationships are a crucial aspect of personhood according to both Scripture and life-span development studies. Yet, change and relationships seem to be in constant tension. During the natural changes of life there is often a cost to be paid. One of the costs of change is the feeling of loneliness.

> Loneliness is experienced in a special developmental way during each stage of the life cycle as the individual struggles to avoid a sense of disenfranchisement and separateness.[4]

Since each era of the life cycle involves changes in self and relationships, loneliness can be experienced at any time in life.

Loneliness may be painfully accompanied by anxiety and emptiness. At different times in life, loneliness is experienced with more peace and assurance. How do persons at different times in life experience loneliness due to the natural changes of life? The emphasis of these paragraphs will be on the "natural loneliness" of life. The traumas and crises which occur outside natural development will be considered in following chapters. Here our focus will be on the loneliness which we face even in the best of times.

The Preschool Child

The preschool child has intense needs for relationships. Parents are the most important companions. The older preschooler will also place importance in grandparents, a teacher, and perhaps a few playmates. The preschooler's loneliness is most likely to be experienced when a parent is not available for comfort and love.

The loneliness of the young child is most dramatically seen when the six- to nine-month-old child is temporarily separated from his parent. He is likely to express his loneliness with tears, anxiety, and anger. His display of emotion is sometimes so great that some parents cannot make themselves leave him with a babysitter. This form of loneliness has been named "separation anxiety."[5] Separation anxiety is characterized by a sharp protest of emotion, either anger or fear. The preschooler's anxiety can become despair and detachment if the primary caregiver is absent either emotionally or physically for an extended period of time. Most children will display this feeling only briefly. Indeed, if the parents will regularly leave the child with a reliable sitter, the child will adjust to their absence with little more than a brief protest.

However, this fear of abandonment lies so deep within the child that threats of abandonment may leave permanent scars. Indeed, young children seem to find their parent's presence nurturing, even when their actions are abusive and unloving. Continuity of care is very important for the young child.

This loneliness is more profoundly experienced by preschoolers who have been physically or emotionally abandoned by their parents and other caregivers. They may be listless with almost no involvement with the external world. Without a parent to "push off from," to say no to, the child has difficulty establishing his own identity. This is the loneliness of an unformed identity.

Preschoolers require another who will stay put when they say, "No! Me do it." When parents feel rushed, they may react angrily to this apparent "stubbornness." However, most often the child is not being stubborn but beginning to express his individuality. He is learning to express himself by doing. Parents need to provide an environment in which the child's needs to do for self can be met while at the same time meeting their own needs to be on time and carry on in their own worlds.

If the child's need to develop a sense of competence is blocked by overhelpful parents, the child is likely to develop an expectation that others will always be there for him. Further, he may feel that he cannot do for himself. Later, when another person is not available to take care of him, he is likely to experience loneliness. In his loneliness he is likely to expect someone else to rescue him.

Already we can see how a balance of aloneness and community must be maintained in order to face life's crisis experiences. The possibility for loneliness cannot be removed from this balance.

The School-Age Child

The school-age child will likely have established his sense of self within his family. However, school, church, and friends demand some separation from the family. The child will experience a longing for the protection and intimacy of the family which will no longer be possible. The child's involvement in educational experiences outside the home may again raise the problems of separation anxiety which seemed to have been left behind in infancy. Some school phobias are examples of this anxiety.

Loneliness may be felt when the newly autonomous school-age child realizes she can no longer be totally dependent on her parents as she once had been. Perhaps this loneliness is illustrated by the seven-year-old who packs a knapsack and "runs away from home," never to get beyond his friend's house around the corner. Parents may find the child seems to demand more letting go than holding on during this time.

The school age child is seldom obviously lonely. One study found that approximately 10 percent of children report feeling lonely.[6] However, they will report being bored, having behavioral problems in school, or strive for attention on the ball field. These behaviors will sometimes be acted-out loneliness. But the child will seldom talk about loneliness.

Hobbies provide one means by which aloneness and togetherness can be balanced. Scout groups, church mission groups, sport teams, and art lessons are some children's activities which push them beyond their family's world and into engagement with other children and with other adults. Children do have significant concerns for having social relationships. They enjoy having friends, being liked, and having someone to play with. Parents and other caregivers must provide opportunities for their children to interact with others.

The Adolescent

A new kind of loneliness begins with adolescence. Many researchers have concluded that adolescence is the time in life when persons are most likely to experience loneliness.[7] Indeed, a certain level of loneliness may be unavoidable during adolescence.

There is good reason for this heightened experience of loneliness. Friendships and interpersonal intimacy become all-important to the adolescent. All persons seek an answer to the question, "With whom do I fit?" But this question is the crux of the adolescent search. When a friendship is broken or betrayed, the very core of the adolescent's self-hood is threatened. Their self-other balance depends upon the holding on of their peers.

In addition, during this time adolescents develop the capacity "to see themselves as others see them." This means that he is likely to judge his worth and value through the eyes of his peer group, through the eyes of those by whom he wants to be valued. When there are signs that he is not being accepted, loneliness is a common response.

The adolescent frequently experiences low self-esteem as a companion of loneliness. Her changing physical shape, skin blemishes, and lack of coordination may produce feelings of inadequacy. These feelings will quickly separate the young person from others. Physical separation leads to loneliness.

But feelings of social isolation may be present even when there are friends available. This is most likely to occur in the person who has totally relied on those around her for a sense of self. That is, some young persons fail to develop an internal identity, a personalized individuality. Their sense of self is totally dependent upon what they see reflected in the faces of others. In the absence of friends, or when those friends are disapproving, the adolescent may experience profound isolation and loneliness. This is one reason that suicide is a difficult problem with adolescents. They frequently are unable to see others truly caring for them and their pain.

The early teen years are usually marked by friendships with two or three "chums." The girl or boy who has difficulty relating with this level of intimacy will feel "left out" or "different." Peer groups begin to influence thoughts and feelings in more profound ways. At some point in adolescence, most young people long more for their peers' acceptance than their family's. Further, since these close friendships will not last forever, deep pains of loneliness are felt when the relationships inevitably separate. The young adolescent is learn-

ing the art of collaboration. Collaboration demands that I allow another to know my inner thoughts and feelings. When there is not
another or when that other leaves, loneliness is unavoidable.

When the chum relationships change to "love" relationships in
mid-adolescence, new opportunities and dangers arise. The opportunity is present for new levels of friendship and companionship. These
experiences provide the building blocks which will later lead to life-
long intimate relationships. Here are the twin dangers of "loosing
myself in another" and of "not having another." Each of these is
tempting. Some are tempted to do anything in order to have another's
acceptance. Others despair because they do not have a close relationship. This pain is evident in the agony of those who "have nothing to
do" on weekend evenings.

> The loneliness of adolescence is a very specific kind of experience
> which arises from the adolescent's personal development as well as
> social demands. The loneliness of adolescence is based on a profound
> awareness of difference and separateness from all others—even their
> families as well as a sense of alienation within their own families.[8]

These longings sometimes push adolescents into behaviors which they
would not rationally choose, but which seem essential in order to
maintain friendships.

The fear of loneliness is a driving force in adolescent life. During
this season we see most clearly a fundamental tension built into human life. This is the tension between community and individuality.
These times of loneliness may be escaped by compulsive activity—
always being with friends, "parties" every weekend, risk-taking behaviors (fast driving, dangerous sports, using drugs), and premature
sexual activity. Or these lonely times may be used to clarify self and
to seek a prayerful integration of self with God. Adult sponsors who
can enable the adolescent to negotiate these rational rapids play an
essential role in the developmental journey.

The Young Adult

Young adulthood brings the loneliness of leaving home and forming one's own expectations for life. The secure if tumultuous world of adolescence yields to the demands of work and marriage. One of the favorite songs of college students is "Lonesome Valley." The words express well the inner conflict of the young adult.

> Jesus walked thislonesome valley,
> He had to walk it by himself;
> O, Nobody else could walk it for Him,
> He had to walk it by Himself.
>
> You must go and stand your trial.
> You have to stand it by yourself;
> Oh, nobody else can stand it for you,
> You have to stand it by yourself.

Although companionship is deeply valued, loneliness in work, play, and love is a frequent experience.

Relationships with key persons and networks of persons are both important. Those who have difficulty making friends may find this season particularly difficult. The key factor in making friends during this period seems to be the capacity for self-disclosure. That is, it is very important that young adults be able to share with others their inner thoughts and feelings. This seems to be especially true for women.

Loneliness can be experienced in both of the key tasks of young adulthood: career and intimacy. The loneliness of persons who give themselves to their career can be very painful. While career satisfaction is important, it does not provide the deep relationships for which persons are created. Sometimes relationships through work can provide such satisfaction. This is not a common experience.

On the other hand, the deep loneliness which pervades many marriages is evidence that simply beginning an intimate relationship does not ensure relief from loneliness. One common false assumption of marriage is that loneliness can be cured by marriage.

> Loneliness cannot be cured by marriage. Loneliness is better tolerated by those who live alone; they have no expectations, and thus no disappointments. Lonely people who live together have about the same chance of realizing their expectations as the host who insists that everyone have a good time at his party.[9]

Both career and marriage may only deepen loneliness. This is true when career is made the entire focus of life. This is true when two lonely people marry with the assumption that togetherness will relieve loneliness. Investing either in career or in marriage may ultimately prove to be ways of avoiding genuine relationships.

Some young adults experience such a deep fear of love that opportunities for intimacy in social relationships, in church, and in work are distorted and lost. Sometimes this fear results in young adults resisting the opportunities for relationships. Their resistance to relationships leads to the feared loneliness. The young adult must understand and undertake the risks of relationship by risking the consequences. A frequent complaint is: "They just want more of me and my time than I want to give." This stance becomes another time of isolated loneliness.

The young adult who feels pulled apart by others and is disenchanted with the "real world" may suffer deep loneliness. The cartoon strip "Cathy" provides numerous expressions of this loneliness.

The Middle Adult

The period of life from forty-five to sixty-five is indeed a time of "being in the middle." Most research indicates that middle adulthood is the least lonely period of life. During this season persons are usually invested in some combination of caring for career, spouse, children, and parents. The middle adult is faced with the stress of giving up independence on behalf of others.

When the middle adult experiences loneliness, it is frequently the loneliness of separation from self. "I have so many demands on me that I don't know who I am anymore." Marriage, parenthood, and society expect the adult to be fully given to others. The boundaries of self which the young adult can maintain are no longer easily maintained. The middle adult feels that he "has no time for myself," or "no one ever calls except when they want something out of me."

Several life crises may threaten one's sense of community and lead to loneliness. Physical and emotional illnesses, unemployment and underemployment, and stresses with one's children or parents may culminate in severe problems and tensions.

The lonely middle adult is particularly vulnerable to stress-related illnesses such as heart disease and anxiety. This is one reason why participation in leisure pastimes is so important. It may be difficult to make time for golf, tennis, walking, knitting, or casual reading. It will be even more difficult to find ways to be involved with new groups of people simply for the sake of enjoyment. However, these activities will be essential if a stress-reducing life-style is to be developed.

Later in middle adulthood, a community of friendships may become more important when the children are no longer living at home. The danger of middle adulthood loneliness may strike when the adult has "given self away." A "mid-life crisis" or "one last fling" may seem to be relief from the burden of loneliness. Thus the middle adult is tempted by sexual relationships which promise a return to the self-giving warmth of young adulthood. Major career changes sometimes result in order to establish some new self-boundaries. Both the self-giving and the return to self are frought with dangers for loneliness. The warm, if unexciting, intimacy of a long-term marriage may be threatened or destroyed. The familiarity of colleagues who have supported an extensive career may be cut off. Yet the excitement of "doing something I really want to do" can sometimes be overpowering. The lonely middle adult will require a caring community to provide support and challenge as these dangers are faced.

The Older Adult

The older adult has received more intensive study in recent years. Since our population will be aging well into the twenty-first century, more intensive geriatric studies will provide even better understandings of this period in life. As the normal life-span increases, we also recognize that there are vast differences within this period. The life issues and needs of the sixty-five, seventy-five, and eighty-five-year-old are very different.

Older adulthood is often thought of as a very lonely time. However, research has shown that it is one of the least lonely life periods.[10] However, for persons who have reduced capacity for activity due to health or lack of financial resources, loneliness is more of a problem. Nevertheless, persons over sixty report less loneliness than any other age group. They seem to be more satisfied with their relationships and to be comfortable being alone. Studies have indicated that compatibility and companionship are indeed valued by older adults. But these values are not as important as a sense of control over their lives and having sufficient resources (safety, transportation, and finances) to feel comfortable.

Nevertheless, isolation among the elderly can be very real. Those who have not made adequate personal and financial plans for old age are most vulnerable to isolation. Those who are unaware of available church, health, and social service resources in the community are also quite vulnerable. For some, this isolation leads to loneliness. Many elderly cope with their isolation through extensive television viewing. Such viewing does aid the isolated in staying in contact with the world in which they live. It also provides opportunities for ongoing learning. But it may be nothing more than a way to pass time when bored or to avoid feelings of loneliness.[11] This behavior does not meet the needs for challenge and relationship which we carry throughout life.

The transition from work to retirement is one of the more vulnerable times for loneliness. Many men and some women have placed their entire sense of worth and effort into their career. They have few friends or activities outside of work. When retirement occurs, they are left with few intimate relationships and little satisfying activity. The newly retired are prime candidates for loneliness.

Another vulnerable time for loneliness is the death of one's spouse or close friends. The sense of desolation which comes with the loss of such intimate attachments can be overwhelming. Their deaths may leave gaps into which loneliness creeps. The death of a spouse may be the most dangerous event for loneliness. This is especially true for relationships in which there was little independence between the spouses. If dependence on each other was great, the surviving spouse is more likely to experience loneliness. In chapter 3 I will more fully explore this close relationship between grief and loneliness.

The unity of the seasons.—There is a loneliness which is rooted in the natural experiences of every person. The seasons of life bring a rhythm of individual and relational changes. These changes follow a general developmental course shared by most persons. We are more alike than we are different in experiencing loneliness as part of the seasons of life. We have seen how the flow of life tends to move from the child's dependence on parents to the older adult's dependence on their children. Times of dependence and times of autonomy flow throughout life. An essential question when pondering your feeling of loneliness may be: "Is my loneliness a natural expression of my current place in life?" Your reflections on this question may not remove your loneliness. Perhaps they will help you keep your pain in perspective.

Growing Through Loneliness

Now I can turn from the pain and promise of developmental loneliness to discuss ways that the promise can be claimed. How can we use this awareness to cope more effectively with loneliness? Are there ways to use this loneliness to grow?

The recognition that loneliness is just part of the human condition can be a freeing knowledge. It is woven into the tapestry of every life. Sometimes my loneliness is not an experience to be fought, changed, or avoided. It is just part of where I am in life. The spiritual gifts of patience and hope are most directly useful here.

Likewise, other persons who are lonely and desperately reach out to me require my compassion and companionship. However, there are times when no amount of companionship will meet their need. One reason for this is that their season in life is a lonely time. They are going through some changes and my presence cannot change that. They may need me, but I dare not expect that I will significantly change their feelings of loneliness. This knowledge may release us from unnecessary worry and effort. There are times when my loneliness will not be relieved. There are times when I will not relieve the loneliness of others. Such is the course of human development.

The growing person cannot escape the threat of loneliness. However, the way this threat is faced determines whether the loneliness will become destructive or merely present. Loneliness becomes an opportunity for growth when we allow the natural rhythms of life to remind us of our connectedness and separation from others. Birthdays, especially key ones such as sixteen, thirty, forty-five, and sixty-five may become times for examining who we are related to and how.

A life-review exercise can help us be prepared for the natural changes which occur. It may also help keep track of changes in key relationships. The following questions may help focus your reflections at crucial life junctures. Create some quiet, alone time and answer these questions, preferably in writing.

1. Whom do I depend upon to help me feel positive about myself, to build up my sense of self-worth?
2. For what and to whom am I now responsible; what roles do I perform for myself and others?
3. Have my images, thoughts, and feelings about God changed in the last year? How is God present or absent to me today?
4. What persons, values, causes, and institutions am I committed to today? Have these changed? To whom do I look for guidance in my choices and life directions?

You may want to share your answers with someone whom you trust. Your spouse, best friend, or pastor may help you gain more perspective on your current life situation. From this perspective you may be ready to confront your loneliness as it is a natural part of your life experience.

Parents would also do well to reflect on their children's lives to better see their loneliness. Our children's loneliness is also an opportunity for their growth. We need to be careful not to quickly push them toward television, music lessons, art lessons, and sports. These activities may help avoid loneliness, but they will not remove those feelings. Of more importance is the number and quality of social relationships our children enjoy. Remember that there is a developmental quality to these relationships. Preschoolers depend most upon their parents. School-age children depend most upon a few same-sex friends. Early adolescents depend most upon a group of like-minded peers. Older adolescents depend most upon a few special friends.

Parents and other caregivers enable children's development best by supporting their involvement with others at their appropriate level of relationship.

"To everything there is a season" is the key truth to a balanced life. There are essential feelings, thoughts, and relationships during every stage of life. However, when persons attempt to maintain these experiences in other stages of life, pain is likely to develop. Frequently this pain is loneliness. Balancing community and individuality is thus a key at every turn of life. The creative power of the Holy Spirit will allow those who strive for this balance to create paths for both intimacy and community.

Most adults will need to attend to continued growth in intimacy with friends and family. Their family may well include parents, siblings, children, and grandchildren. Thus, family enrichment activities are appropriate for meeting the needs of adults who tend to experience loneliness. Adults without families may need to develop ties to other families so that similar levels of intimacy can be attained.

Middle adults anticipating retirement and older adults who have retired will want to attend to some specific issues relevant to their time in life. Three attitudes are particularly important in feeling satisfied with self and relationships during this time.[12] First, those who are more willing to seek challenges are less likely to experience loneliness. Second, those who have visible responsibilities and achievements are more likely to be satisfied with life. Third, those who feel positive about their family relationships are less likely to feel lonely and more likely to be satisfied with life. You will do well to evaluate your own attitudes in these areas. In areas where you are weak, you will want to develop more positive attitudes.

Those who are interested in older adults will also attend to these needed attitudes. It is important for older adults to be supported in attempting new ventures and learning new skills. It is important that their communities, such as churches, utilize their energies and skills in visible and productive ways. Older adults need to continue to grow individually and relationally.

Loneliness is an expected experience throughout the seasons of life. This chapter has explored the loneliness naturally present to all of us during critical junctures in life. Further, I have discussed how time brings changes. Change brings with it the threat of the pain of separation. To let go of the old and grasp onto the new is risky. The fabric of life is woven with the threat of loneliness. When we rigidly avoid loneliness we are likely avoiding the pain of growth and life. A balance of community and relationship is essential to the growing person. Identity, community, and vocation require both aloneness and relationships. We seek graceful relationships with others and the grace of God in experiencing both the pain and promise of loneliness throughout the seasons of life.

Notes

1. Walter Brueggemann, *The Hopeful Imagination* (Philadelphia: Fortress Press, 1986), pp. 1-7.

2. Robert Kegan, *The Evolving Self* (Cambridge, Mass.: Harvard University Press, 1982), pp. 73-85.

3. Kegan, pp. 115-132.

4. Samuel M. Natale, *Loneliness and Spiritual Growth* (Birmingham, Ala.: Religious Education Press, 1986), p. 72.

5. John Bowlby, "Affectional Bonds: Their Nature and Origin," *The Experience of Loneliness: Studies in Emotional and Social Isolation,* ed. Robert S. Weiss (Cambridge, Mass.: MIT Press, 1973), pp. 38-52. See also John Bowlby, *Separation: Anxiety and Anger* (New York: Basic Books, 1973).

6. Steven R. Asher, S. Hymel, and P. Renshaw, "Loneliness in Children," *Child Development,* 55 (1984), pp. 1456-1464.

7. Tim Brennan, "Loneliness at Adolescence," *Loneliness: A Sourcebook of Current Theory, Research, and Therapy,* eds. Letitia Peplau and Daniel Perlman (New York: Wiley and Sons, 1982), pp. 269-290.

8. Natale, *Loneliness,* p. 82.

9. William J. Lederer and Don D. Jackson, *The Mirages of Marriage* (New York: Norton, 1968), p. 78.

10. Letitia Peplau, et al., "Loneliness: Antecedents and Coping Strategies in the Lives of Widows," *Loneliness,* pp. 327-347.

11. Ostman and D. Jeffers, "Life Stage and Motives for Television Use," *International Journal of Ageing and Human Development,* 17 (1983), pp. 315-322.

12. M. W. Steinkamp and J. R. Kelly, "Relationships Among Motivational Orientation, Level of Leisure Activity, and Life Satisfaction in Older Men and Women," *Journal of Psychology,* 119 (1985), pp. 509-520.

3

Emotional Loneliness
and Nurture

Jane enjoyed a close relationship with her next-door neighbor, Linda. No one was surprised then when Jane "could not get over" Linda's rather untimely death. Jane had never felt such emptiness. In contrast, Bill had many friends yet also felt "empty." He tried many ways to motivate himself, yet he found life less and less pleasurable. He had increasing difficulty reaching out to people he thought were very close to him. Jane was experiencing the pain of grief while Bill was struggling through the depths of depression. These are just two of the many emotional struggles which include loneliness.

One difficulty in understanding and coping with loneliness is that it usually is accompanied by other painful feelings. Also, loneliness is frequently a part of other emotions. For example, depression, grief, and despair are frequent companions of loneliness. Thus, we must understand these emotions in order to see all the textures of loneliness. However, we must not confuse these emotions with loneliness. There is a wide spectrum of emotional vulnerability to loneliness.

Clinical research has identified emotions most likely to accompany loneliness. The lonely person is likely to feel one or more of these emotions: depression, isolation, emptiness, frustration, and anxiety.[1] Each of these feelings can be further defined. A depressed person may feel sad, worthless, unmotivated, hopeless, and guilty. An isolated person may feel deserted and friendless. An empty person is likely to feel no sense of life purpose or life direction. A frustrated person may feel angry and lacking in the ability to achieve life goals. An anxious person may be fearful of others, life events, and unable to cope with life's changes.

All of these feelings may be present when the person is lonely. Thus, the person who expresses frustration with life may well be experiencing loneliness. On the other hand, frustration is not always a part of loneliness. Just because these emotions are present does not mean that loneliness is definitely the problem. This may sound like "double-talk." However, if the person who is emotionally distressed and lonely is to find help, we must be careful to see the similarities and differences between various emotional experiences which appear similar and do overlap.

Emotional conditions (depression, anxiety, frustration) and loneliness frequently coincide when there are problems within oneself. Some persons experience an inner emptiness, a personal void, which leaves them vulnerable to the pain of loneliness. This inner emptiness is then drawn out when stress or trauma invades one's life. The opposite of this is true as well. Loneliness is seldom experienced when one has a positive self-concept and physical vigor.[2]

In what ways do persons who are under emotional stress begin to also experience loneliness? Some of the signs that an emotional experience may turn to loneliness include apprehensiveness, anxiety, oversensitive vigilance, and a sense of utter aloneness.[3] The apprehensive or vigilant person is likely to say, "I feel so bad, and those people seem ready to hurt me; I'll keep away from them." Or, "I was hurt once before when I felt this way, so I just will not risk being with people again." The anxious person is likely to be so inwardly shaken that he cannot realize enough personal freedom to reach out to others. The alone person tends to say something like, "I do not like myself; I do not like others; I will not be in contact with others."

Studies have not been able to identify either depression or loneliness as the cause of the other.[4] This is true for other emotional conditions as well. Thus, loneliness and depression are somewhat like twins. They are often confused, especially when they show up in the same place at the same time. Loneliness, depression, grief, anxiety, and despair are related yet different experiences. This chapter will describe these painful experiences and offer guidance in better coping with the loneliness which accompanies them.

Scriptural teachings on the emotions.—Scripture certainly describes the close connection between loneliness and painful human emotions. For example, during the dark days of Job's suffering, he begged his friends to leave him. The emotional complex of grief and the pain of his illness led Job to seek solitude. "Let me alone, for my days are a breath" (Job. 7:16). A frequent cry of those who suffer is: "Leave me alone!" Sometimes when those in grief and pain are left alone, they experience the pangs of loneliness. Job's friends were caring enough not to leave him. Unfortunately, their care of him was not very helpful. But he at least did not have to endure his suffering alone.

However, sometimes we do need to be alone in our emotional pain. Loneliness is not always present during such a time of aloneness. During a time of political upheaval, the writer of Lamentations was in great agony as he surveyed the distress of the people of Jerusalem. They were suffering under the occupation of yet another foreign power. He counseled that grief and affliction are to be born in solitude. "Let him sit alone in silence / when he [God] has laid it on him" (Lam. 3:28). Aloneness is sometimes required as a sign of submission and penitence when we are faced with the truth of God's righteousness. At such times we are called to a deep look within and self-understanding which require solitude for formation. Sometimes emotional pain calls for aloneness.

Both Job and the writer of Lamentations were faced with complex situations. Their situations created difficult emotional experiences of grief, despair, and fear. Scripture indicates that solitude may be a natural solace at such times. However, solitude sometimes leads to loneliness. Since loneliness itself may create severely painful feelings, a vicious circle may emerge which drives the sufferer ever deeper into the depths of a pit.

The task of deciding when emotional loneliness calls for solitude and when it calls for companionship is difficult. Job's friends may well have seen his emotional exhaustion, anger, and fatigue and responded by not leaving him alone. On the other hand, the writer of Lamentations may have been writing about a time in which vigor and self-direction were well established. Thus loneliness would not have been as much of a threat. He could risk being alone in his pain.

The Emotional Pain of Loneliness

The modern-day stories of many people are full of painful loneliness. For example, Vietnam veterans frequently told of the shock of being injured severely, having good friends killed, and of coming home to an ungrateful family and community. The deep pains of isolation, injured bodies, and wounded spirits sometimes built to unbearable proportions. Loneliness becomes a way of life that drives away loving wives, confused children, and disappointed friends. Anger, frustration, and depression become daily companions which deepen their isolation.

Others who have experienced deep trauma—victims of natural disasters, accident victims, and assault victims—will identify with these painful experiences. One of the most important and difficult acts in recovering from deep trauma is to remain connected to one's community. The deeper danger for the trauma victim who becomes isolated is that her ever-deepening pain cannot be adequately cared for.

Perhaps four basic categories of feelings can summarize the interconnectedness of loneliness and emotional pain.[5] These feelings are frequently present when a person is lonely. They are also likely to lead the person to feel even more lonely. (1) "Desperation" includes feelings of panic, helplessness, fear, abandonment, and vulnerability. (2) "Boredom" includes feelings such as a desire to be elsewhere, uneasiness, anger, and inability to concentrate on the present. (3) "Self-deprecation" includes feelings of being unattractive, stupid, ashamed, and insecure. (4) "Depression" is characterized by sadness, emptiness, feeling sorry for oneself, and melancholy. These four feelings will help keep in focus the many dimensions of emotional loneliness.

Many events may stir the tragic combinations of emotional distress and loneliness. However, three complex experiences seem most likely to place a person in the difficult experience of both loneliness and emotional distress. These experiences include grief, depression, and physical illness. I must emphasize that not everyone who is grieving or depressed will also be lonely. Many will be. I will discuss these tragic problems with an eye to both the pain and promise involved in each.

Loneliness and Grief

Loneliness and grief may be the most familiar combination of emotional distress and longing for a relationship. Grief which follows the death of a spouse clearly illustrates this principle. One study found that up to 86 percent of widows reported deep loneliness following their spouse's death. When children are available for support, this percentage does drop somewhat.[6] Indeed, the absence of both marital companion and social support is most painful. Loneliness is frequently present in grief and is made more intense when social isolation accompanies grief. The combination of grief and isolation is particularly painful and frightening.

The grieving go through many experiences which seem to create tension between knowing the person is gone and wanting the relationship to continue. For example, sometimes a grieving wife will go on "seeing" her deceased husband for several months following his death. She may even carry on conversations, fix his favorite meals, and go to their special places in order to escape the deep pain of grief and terror of loneliness.

Grief which follows a divorce may be equally traumatic and lead to just as intense loneliness. Confronting this pain may open up new avenues for healing. One woman tells a story of hatred for her divorced husband who had taken their old house and left her to fend for herself. Her adult children were equally bitter. Yet as the first Christmas approached following the divorce, she knew that her grief over the loss of her marriage had led to unhealthy bitterness. Her grief had also isolated her from supportive personal and church communities. Even more important, her deepest values of forgiveness and hope were being drained away by her grief and loneliness. In order to confront her grief directly she invited her former husband to Christmas dinner! While all their children struggled to deal with their own feelings upon finding their father again involved in the family on Christmas Day, both her grief and loneliness were finally faced. There is no fairy tale ending. They remained divorced, the children remained confused, and he eventually remarried. Nevertheless, she was no longer lonely, and her grief was well on the way to healing.[7]

The human roots of this association between grief and loneliness are not difficult to understand. When we suffer a pain, one protective step we may take is to limit our contact with others, so no one else can hurt us. This isolation may reinforce our negative thoughts and feelings about self and others. The psychologist Karen Horney has written, "Emotional isolation is hard for anyone to endure; it becomes a calamity, however, if it coincides with apprehensions and uncertainties about one's self."[8] The traumas of grief associated with death and divorce can certainly lead one to struggle with self-doubt. Such isolation may then bring deep loneliness which is extremely difficult to face.

Another kind of grief is more difficult to see. But it is even more powerful in leading us into loneliness. This is unresolved grief. Unresolved grief refers to an ongoing experience of grief which is responding to a loss more than two or three years previous. For example, the death of a young child's parent may leave deep wounds which fester as loneliness for many years. This loneliness may result in creation of imaginary conversations and in treasuring the few memories left from childhood. However, this loneliness may also result in even deeper problems. The child may not be able to establish new loving relationships because of his ongoing grief. Professional counselors know that clinical depression is much more prevalent among adults who lost a parent through death in childhood. Again, we see the connection between deep emotions and the experience of loneliness.

The Bible and grief.—There certainly are times when being alone with one's grief is helpful. Job found comfort in being alone in his grief. "Are not the days of my life few? / Let me alone that I may find a little comfort / before I go whence I shall not return" (Job 10:20-21*a*). Aloneness was important, so he could face the inevitability of grief and death. He was thus able to express his weariness directly to God. Aloneness may be healing for grief. But loneliness complicates the healing process.

At times our strong emphasis on individual identity and responsibility may lead to loneliness. I sometimes hear from a grieving person, "This is just a burden I will have to bear by myself." While there is truth to this sentiment, aloneness is not the whole story. When facing the loneliness of grief from the death of a loved one, persons may find comfort in the Christian conviction that the individual's identity and personhood extends beyond death.[9] "The communion of the saints" may provide both presence and hope for those who are grieving.

Numerous Scriptures help us see that, though a loved one is not physically with us, they are yet alive. In Mark 9:2-8 we find Jesus' experience of "transfiguration." He was taken into a nonearthly situation and talked with Elijah and Moses. The passage teaches us that Jesus is indeed the Messiah sent by God. It also teaches that personal identity survives death. In Luke 16:19-31 we read Jesus' parable of the rich man and Lazarus. The focus of the passage is an urgent need for repentance no matter what our outward circumstances in life. It also teaches us that those who die have an individual, personal destiny.

Those in grief may sometimes lose sight of these truths. While we no longer have physical companionship, we expect a day of companionship in God's future. This hope does not eliminate the pain of grief now. Indeed, seldom does it help to remind those who grieve intensely of these scriptural promises. This is a time for comfort rather than instruction. However, the promises do put such pain in the perspective of the kingdom of God. As believers we can be assured of never being completely alone, regardless of the depth and extent of our grief.

Loneliness and Depression

Clinical depression is a powerful and tragic illness which sometimes accompanies loneliness. It may also lead to loneliness. We must carefully distinguish depression and "the blues." It is common to speak of "being depressed" when we feel sad, slowed down, and unmotivated. All these feelings accompany loneliness. Usually "being down" is not clinical depression. Clinical depression involves these feelings to such depth that eating and sleeping patterns are changed, sexual energies are depleted, thoughts become disorganized, and common activities can be completed only with great difficulty. I will focus here on the severe form of depression although much of the information will be applicable to "feeling blue" as well.

Joyce's husband had died almost one year previously. Her friends thought she had made a good adjustment to living alone after thirty-nine years of marriage. She had stayed active in church. Her daughter, Jane, lived nearby, visited regularly, and felt good about her mother's adjustment. However, Jane realized that Joyce was no longer going to the book discussions at the library or to the women's group at church; she was not even coming to visit her grandchildren with any regularity. When she asked Joyce what was happening, Joyce brushed her off with "I have just gotten tired." Jane accepted this response for a few weeks until she became aware that her mother was losing weight, not keeping her apartment neat, and was hardly getting out of bed. Joyce moved through her period of grief and had made a good adjustment to her husband's death. However, she had fallen into depression. Depression often goes unrecognized for long periods of time, particularly in the elderly.

Both loneliness and depression are characterized by feelings of sadness, anger, guilt, worthlessness, and helplessness. It is frequently difficult to determine whether the person is depressed, lonely, or both. However, loneliness seldom involves the total giving up of hope and self-direction which characterizes depression. Loneliness implies some energy for the search for a companion rather than abandonment of that ideal.[10] The depressed person will usually have given up the longing to have a companion. The despair of loneliness is rooted in faith that companionship is yet possible. The two experiences can be further distinguished by noting that loneliness is a drive to interaction while depression is a pull into withdrawal.[11]

Loneliness may lead into depression. Susan had always felt herself to be a little different from others. Although she had friends, she never felt like she was really a part of any group. Susan seldom offered herself for relationships and expected to be left out of invitations. She did not like the way she looked nor think herself smart enough to do anything more than routine tasks, and she did not believe she had anything to offer to others. She suffered from both low self-esteem and lack of self-confidence. When she was twenty-five,

Susan began to have difficulty falling asleep, stopped eating regular meals, became increasingly lethargic, and separated herself from the few friends she cared for. The combination of loneliness and low self-esteem had led to a major depressive experience.

A danger of clinical depression is that suicide attempts often occur. One trait that many who attempt suicide share is that they are convinced that no one really cares or that others would be better off without them. Occasionally, the suicide attempt is a desperate attempt to get someone to notice them. The similarity of these feelings with those of the intensely lonely is clear. One study found that those seasons of the year when persons are most likely to make suicide attempts (winter and spring) are also the times when persons report greatest feelings of loneliness.[12] I am not suggesting that lonely people are more likely to attempt suicide. I am saying that depression and loneliness may combine with dangerous outcomes.

The Bible and depression.—I have not been able to identify any specific scriptural situations in which the person was clearly suffering from what is now called depression. Certainly they experienced grief (Ruth), feelings of separation from God (David), and unwillingness to do the task at hand (Jonah). King Saul certainly struggled with an emotional disorder which had some symptoms that may remind us of depression. But none of these situations are described in such a way that we can clearly think of them as depression.

Nevertheless, Scripture does provide insight into this interaction between loneliness and depression. First, the true nature of love is made very clear. First John 4:7-8 says, "Beloved, let us love one another; for love is of God, and he who loves is born of God and knows God. He who does not love does not know God; for God is love." Our energy for relationships begins in God's love. God's love in us is proven by our relationships with others. Those who suffer from depression and loneliness know the pain of not feeling these relationships to be present. They therefore require from others the deep love and care which demonstrates that God's "love is perfected in us" (1 John 4:12).

Second, the depressed and lonely may rely upon scriptural promises of the constant love of God, regardless of their feelings or circumstances. "By day the Lord commands his steadfast love; / and at night his song is with me, / a prayer to the God of my life" (Ps. 42:8). God accepts us and loves us, whatever our life situation. Bible reading, prayer, and focusing on God's love may not cure depression, but they can keep depression from turning into a spiritual crisis.

When we care for those who are lonely and depressed, we must be careful not to attempt to encourage, cajole, or demand them out of their feelings. Depression has complex causes which are likely both physical and emotional. Depressed persons require trained medical and psychological assessment. Friends and pastors are important in recognizing the signs of depression and helping the persons to seek out the help they need. The sooner this is done, the quicker the cure can be, and the less suffering the person will go through.

In addition, friends can be good listeners, especially if they resist the temptation to try "to fix" their depressed friend. No one can solve a depressed and lonely person's emotional problems. Depressed persons do not need advice, they need presence and a listening ear. It is especially important to care for your friend by identifying the feelings you hear expressed, no matter how painful they may be. Remember to listen carefully rather than to lecture or condemn.

Loneliness and Physical Illness

Physical illness is often accompanied by loneliness. Loneliness may also be the cause of some physical illnesses. Illness may involve a time of isolation from others which leads to a desire for more relationships. A longing for more relationships may lead to physical illness. This interaction between body and emotion should come as no surprise for Christians who affirm the wholeness of persons.

Loneliness resulting from physical illness.—When serious illness disrupts our life routines, we feel cut off from church, from work, and sometimes even from family. Hospitals, nursing homes, and rehabilitation centers are full of lonely people. During a time of difficulty, the Psalmist offered this prayer:

> Turn thou to me, and be gracious to me;
> for I am lonely and afflicted.
> Relieve the troubles of my heart,
> and bring me out of my distresses (Ps. 25:16-17).

Many persons suffering from serious illnesses have prayed similar prayers. "Troubles of my heart" and "afflicted" seem intertwined. Illness and loneliness frequently accompany each other.

Loneliness is even further increased when the illness requires physical isolation. A few illnesses in the modern medical center require this kind of isolation. Patients in intensive care units usually have very limited contact with people other than busy medical personnel. Some infections require very limited exposure to others.

Some cultures have isolated certain ill people from the rest of society. Leviticus 13 provided the biblical basis for the isolation of lepers in early Jewish society. In our day, patients with Acquired Immunodeficiency Syndrome (AIDS) may experience this same isolation. Indeed, some communities have sought to exclude persons who have been exposed to the virus even though they presently show no symptoms of the illness. One ministry of the church throughout history was to the leper colonies. Now that disease has been almost conquered. The church may be called to offer similar communities of support for the lonely AIDS patient.

Sometimes the ill have been isolated because it was believed their illness was a result of their sin. Psalm 38 is grounded in the belief that the psalmist's grave illness was a result of his sin. "There is no soundness in my flesh because of thy indignation; / there is no health in my bones because of my sin" (Ps. 38:3). His friends had abandoned him. "My friends and companions stand aloof from my plague, / and my kinsmen stand afar off" (Ps. 38:11). The psalmist pleaded with God to be near and not to forsake him as his friends had done.

Job received much the same treatment from his friends. They encouraged him to confess his sins, so God could forgive him and restore him. Illness and sin both lead to isolation. When the two are combined, deep loneliness may emerge. But healing is always a hope. Those who are tormented by physical pain and by loneliness look to God for strength and healing.

> Hear my cry, O Lord;
> let my cry come to thee!
> Do not hide thy face from me
>   in the day of my distress!
> Incline thy ear to me;
> answer me speedily in the day
>   when I call! (Ps. 102:1-2).

Both illness and loneliness are occasions when we may grow closer to God. Today we do not attempt to isolate the ill unless it is essential for public health. Nor do we assume that illness is the result of sin and thus a form of God's punishment. Physical illness may still be an occasion for self-examination and for seeking a deeper relationship with God.

Jesus searched for those who were ill and alone. One such person who caught Jesus' attention was the man by the pool of Bethesda (John 5:2-18). The lame man could never reach the healing waters because he had no companions to help him into the pool. Jesus befriended the ill man and healed him of his disease. Jesus then concluded the conversation with a caution to the man. He was told to care for his life for there are worse events than becoming ill. There are worse dangers to fulfilled Christian living than illness. This is true of loneliness as well. But illness and loneliness do provide stumbling blocks to fulfillment.

In another New Testament experience, Peter was called to the home of Dorcas who became sick and died (Acts 9:36-43). Scripture notes that she was full of good works and charity. Her death was not the result of sin. When Peter heard of this calamity, he organized a prayer vigil. But Peter prayed alone. In the face of illness and death, solitude and prayer may have amazing results. Upon Peter's prayer, the woman rose from her bed. While aloneness may be destructive, especially when combined with illness, there are occasions where solitude is essential for the working of God's Spirit. Peter used this principle in relation to Dorcas.

Physical illness resulting from loneliness.—Medical research has demonstrated that loneliness can have serious medical consequences. Anxiety, migraine headaches, ulcers, hypertension, and heart disease have been related to living alone or to loneliness. Dr. James Lynch in *The Broken Heart: The Medical Consequences of Loneliness* has made a particularly strong case for this relationship. "Cancer, tuberculosis, suicide, accidents, mental disease—all are significantly influenced by human companionship. Nature uses many weapons to shorten the lives of lonely people."[13]

Other researchers have attempted to identify the ways in which loneliness makes one more vulnerable to disease. One study found that the lonely tend to have less ability to ward off illnesses because their immune systems were significantly suppressed.[14] The body's ability to defend itself against disease organisms is lowered when nurturing companions are not available.

Other studies found that a person's quality of social relationships is generally more important than quantity of relationships. That is, we need intimate relationships, even if they are few, more than we need large numbers of friendly people.[15] Thus, illness and death are more likely for those who do not enjoy close friends and relatives, church membership, informal group participation, and a supportive marriage.[16] Warm, intimate relationships are essential for physical health. Again, this conclusion should not surprise those who affirm the wholistic power of human nature.

The interaction between being alone, feeling lonely, and one's health is a delicate balance. This problem will be studied in more depth in the next chapter. Here it is important to see the depth of human pain and disease with which loneliness is associated.

From Loneliness to Nurture

How can the emotionally lonely person move from pain to the promise of nurture? Your movement from emotional pain to the promise of emotional nurture is a difficult journey. Your sense of desperation may tempt you to flee into relationships in order to solve your inner hurt. Your boredom may distract you from the gifts which are very much present. Putting yourself down may tempt you to hide from others and miss the relationships you long for most. Your depression may limit your energy for change and risk taking.

Too often, lonely persons assume that if just the right relationships can be established, they will no longer be lonely. Loneliness which is rooted in the emotional hungers described in this chapter will not be fully satisfied through relationships. Our restless hearts must not be allowed to rush toward others until our inner lives have been fed and strengthened. The emotional hungers of loneliness will likely drive others away or do violence to them instead of nurturing our inner selves.

There is an old story about a man who lost his house keys. A friend came along, asked his problem, and promptly joined the man on his hands and knees looking frantically under the street lamp for the keys. After a thorough search turned up no keys the friend asked, "Where did you lose your keys?" The man replied, "I lost them inside my house." The friend was quite upset. "Then why are we looking here under the street lamp?" The man replied, "Because there is more light here than in my house."

The lonely who are emotionally starved must resist the temptation to look outside of themselves for nurture. Their real need is to turn inward, to go into their own houses, and search for the keys to their loneliness there.

I will offer some strategies for coping with emotional loneliness. Short-term strategies are more likely to be temporary "bandages" which will enable the severely distressed to get through the immediate crisis. Long-term strategies are more likely to deal with the root problems and decrease occasions of loneliness. Both will focus on ways that you can increase your inward sense of nurture and hope.

Short-term Strategies

Short-term strategies begin by taking very seriously the lonely person's emotional pain. When you are grieving, depressed, and emotionally empty, you know that quick words are little comfort. "Cheer up, you will get over this." "Come on! Shake out of it. You can make friends." "Jesus is the only friend you really need, and you know He is here with you." These sentiments may be true. However, as just words, they are not helpful. You are likely to desire a much more patient and nurturing person to offer you support and comfort. You are also likely to need to be patient and nurturing to yourself.

Grief.—If you are grieving and lonely, your main task is "letting go." There is a very real danger for those who begin new love relationships before this letting go has been completed. Too many persons run from the loneliness of grieving over a divorce by too quickly entering new love relationships. They may not suffer immediate pain. There is a high likelihood that they will suffer pain in the future. Most people are not capable of making wise choices for intimate relationships until after the painful working through process has occurred.

You are likely to enjoy a very delicate balance of aloneness and support from people who care for you. Part of the grief process involves letting go of attachments to the person who has died or left. While these attachments are being released, new attachments are difficult to form clearly. Thus, your grief and pain of separation must be fully experienced.

The time period for letting go is highly individual and situational. Some may be prepared for new relationships within three or four months. Others may not be ready for two or three years. However, the loneliness of grief is most likely to last for at least one year. Probably the most important virtue you can live by during this time of letting go is *patience*. If your loneliness lasts more than two years, and you still do not feel ready to engage others, you may be "stuck" in your grief process. In such a situation, you will do well to discuss with your pastor or other trusted person ways that you can be more involved with others.

Scripture offers another helpful perspective at this point as well. The apostle Paul clearly expected the early church to respond to the grieving. In 1 Timothy 5:5, Paul discussed the classes of widows and the church's expectations of each. The widow who is indeed all alone and has no personal resources is to receive special attention and support from the church. Those who are not so alone are expected to be supported by their family and friends. This example indicates how aloneness in grief is to be both respected and ministered to by the church. Those who are alone in grief should be cared for by the church so that loneliness does not result.

Depression.—If you are depressed and lonely, you need to see a physician immediately. Depression is a curable disease, but it is also a deadly disease. Medications may be prescribed which offer relief from the symptoms of depression. The sooner depression is diagnosed and treated, the quicker relief can be expected. The longer depression goes untreated, the more the danger grows that you can seriously harm yourself and your relationships. Trust your companions who support the recommendations of physicians and counselors.

Once treatment begins, you will likely be encouraged to explore your thoughts and feelings which led to depression. This may require such activities as completing a life review, keeping a daily journal, and looking more deeply within yourself for life direction. These activities will force you to come to terms with your own emotional makeup which led to your depression. This is a painful task. Indeed, the early stages of therapy for depression may increase both hope and pain simultaneously.

Allow your friends to encourage you for patience and endurance. You may have little of either during this time. They may also offer living reminders that there is more to God's world than the pain of loneliness and depression.

Physical illness.—If you are chronically ill and lonely, you may be quite dependent upon others to support you. This is also true if you are critically ill and lonely. Yet those who are critically ill may soon return to their normal activities and no longer feel lonely. Your loneliness is situational. The chronically ill person may have to make fundamental changes in life-style. When your unique emotional makeup combines with this difficult situation, deep loneliness may result.

The physically ill person's sense of loneliness is often rooted in an experience of body failure. Changes in appearance, mobility, and competence can shatter your sense of self-worth. It is important that ill persons learn to cope with these feelings of failure, build a new sense of identity, and maintain community, so loneliness does not become a dominating force. Your work to come to terms with limitations is difficult. It will require both inner strength and support from your caring community. However, many chronically ill people have maintained deep and meaningful relationships. You may stay connected to others by telephone calls and letter writing. There are many ways of being of service to others through the telephone and letters. Further, some chronically ill persons find a deep sense of purpose by praying regularly for their church, missionaries, and others. Chronic illness need not lead you into loneliness.

Creative activities.—A short-term strategy appropriate to all of the situations of loneliness is to engage in creative activities. One whose inner life is full of positive interests is very unlikely to ever feel very lonely, whatever the outward circumstances. One way to deal with loneliness is to involve yourself in a new activity or resume an activity abandoned earlier in life.

Creative activities may involve both the world of nature and the world of objects. The world of nature provides many creative and nurturing places. The person who has creative places which nurture the inner self is unlikely to feel lonely, unless deprived of those places. For some it may be the large oak tree in the park around the corner which provides an ongoing sense of place and peace. For others it may be the beach at the lake or ocean, the ridge near a mountain retreat, or the old farmhouse built by grandfather. When loneliness stirred by grief, depression, or illness becomes too heavy, a return to these places may bring comfort.

Sometimes these places cannot be returned to except by memories and pictures. But as long as they can be returned to, they provide creative and powerful memories which give an inner sense of place. Your sense of place is a powerful deterrent to loneliness. Thus, one creative activity is to develop important places which nurture an inner companionship.

Other creative activities focus more on the objects of life. These vary enormously depending upon interests and aptitudes. Arts activities such as poetry, painting, pottery, and sculpture give many lonely people a sense of purpose and companionship. Participation in performing arts such as music, dance, and drama provide others with direction and release. Even listening to music or going to art galleries, although passive, may fill a need for creative involvement. Constructive projects in woodworking, auto repair, or house remodeling give a sense of accomplishment and relationship to things. Intellectual endeavors such as reading, computer programming, and attending community education classes give a similar sense of creative involvement in the ongoing flow of life. The key to all these events is participation. The more you participate in creative activities, the less likely you are to experience loneliness.

A caution is also necessary. It is dangerous for you to participate much in passive activities. Such pastimes as movie going, television watching, and attending sporting events will not usually meet your need for creative involvement with life. In moderation these activities are fine. However, when they limit your active participation in creative projects, they are hindering rather than supporting your openness to nurture.

You will also want to consider the strategy of helping others. Emotional emptiness can sometimes be directly confronted when the less fortunate are remembered. The social needs of our land cry out for those who will volunteer to work in projects which feed the hungry and house the homeless. The political needs of our nation call for persons who will give time and energy to work for peace, justice, and compassion. The religious needs of persons plead for those who will introduce friends and strangers to Christ and sustain the work of churches.

I am well aware that if you are emotionally empty, you may have great difficulty motivating yourself to volunteer for such projects. However, if you begin such projects, relief from loneliness is a likely result.

A biblical example of this is found in 2 Kings 4:8-37. This is the account of the prophet Elijah's experiences with a Shunammite husband and wife who had no children. In their culture, this situation was a sign of lack of favor from God. We could well imagine the longing experienced by this wealthy couple and the dread with which they held their approaching old age. Nevertheless, they offered Elijah food and housing. In spite of their own emptiness they were creatively involved with others. Their pattern is one we are all called to follow. Not all will experience the same miracle which this family received. But the value of offering service will be discovered by all who are able to respond.

Loneliness may be a prompter to become involved in the creative aspects of human living. Creativity may be expressed through nature, projects, or helping others. Grief, depression, and illness are powerful motivators which turn us back onto our own selves. Emotional loneliness may certainly tempt us to salve our pain with passive activities which demand nothing from us. However, creative living is a wonderful short-term strategy for meeting loneliness rooted in emotional emptiness.

Long-term Strategies

The lonely who wish to claim the promise of nurture will also need to develop long-term strategies for their lives. Long-term strategies begin with developing greater satisfaction in being oneself. Persons who lack self-confidence and assume no one else is interested in them are unlikely to experience deeper community. There are three crucial long-term strategies to facing the loneliness of emotional pain. These include developing self-esteem, growing in emotional maturity, and enjoying aloneness. Each of these strategies are built on the conviction that we can change.

All of these strategies have in common the same first step. The lonely person must accept responsibility for his own loneliness. It is very easy to blame your surroundings and circumstances for your feelings. Only those who are willing to stop focusing on their situation and concentrate on their own resources will change enough to creatively face their loneliness.

Once this first step has been taken, there are other important steps which allow us to more adequately face life, whatever our surroundings. You need not be satisfied with simply "coping" with that painful condition. Transformation is possible.

It is difficult to say how others can help you during your journey through these changes. Your friends and Christian companions will certainly be available to enable you to change. However, facing and growing from emotional loneliness is usually an individual journey. The Christian conviction is that we are called, redeemed, and resurrected as individuals. We stand as individuals in both sin and salvation. Some forms of loneliness can be creatively faced only as an individual.[17] Let us take a closer look at the key strategies for facing emotional loneliness.

Self-esteem.—The person who suffers from low self-esteem may well experience loneliness as well. Self-esteem refers to the person's accurate judgment of their value and worth both to others and to God. A painful personal history may make self-esteem very low. At other times an intense dislike for one's body or one's social situation may lead to a struggle with adequate self-esteem. Christians in particular may sometimes struggle with maintaining adequate self-esteem. Our awareness of our failures may be so great that we forget that God loves us regardless of our failures. We may also miss the importance of healthy self-love if we are to love others.

Scripture encourages us to have a high view of our worth, especially when we have been tested. For example, we read in Hebrews, "Therefore do not throw away your confidence, which has a great reward. For you have need of endurance, so that you may do the will of God and receive what is promised" (10:35-36). But our sense of value is always to be held with caution. Paul wrote, "I bid every one among you not to think of himself more highly than he ought to think, but to think with sober judgment, each according to the measure of faith which God has assigned him" (Rom. 12:3). Paul went on in this passage to remind us that every person has a spiritual gift and a function to be exercised within the church. None are to disparage their own gifts to the work of Christ. Certainly none should demean the value of others' gifts.

The first step in building self-esteem is to trust the resources one has. All persons have resources for living creatively in this world. As a lonely person with low self-esteem, you may have great difficulty identifying your resources. You may need to talk with a close friend, trusted parent, teacher, pastor, or vocational guidance counselor. They can help you gain perspective on what talents, positive traits, and inner resources you bring to life. Realistic appraisal is essential at this point. One who is too proud or too meek will cut off opportunities for genuine self-appraisal. When those opportunities are lost, healthy self-esteem will also be lost.

A second step involves risking the use of those resources. You may struggle to plan ahead in order to be prepared for opportunities for solitude and community. You may also find it difficult to take initiative toward the persons and goals you value in life. However, when you experience your power to do what you have intended to do, genuine esteem begins to grow. When the lonely person decides what is important and pursues those goals, self-esteem increases dramatically.

A third step in building self-esteem is to use humor. Humor creates a healthy sense of self. A man who takes himself too seriously is likely to be lonely. A woman with low self-esteem may be unable to see the humor in life events and problems. A person with low self-esteem may be particularly sensitive to signs of failure. If I feel inadequate and unworthy I see failure darkly. The more serious I become about change, about making friends, about any significant goal, the less likely I am to be able to accomplish that change, to make a friend, to reach a goal. I must accept the fact that nobody, including me, is perfect. This conviction is essential if you are to build healthy self-esteem. Humor is a key step in this direction.

Emotional growth.—Those who suffer from emotional loneliness can generally be described as "emotionally empty." One reason these persons long for relationships is that they need growth within themselves. Sometimes this loneliness and need for growth is related to the developmental season of the person, as described in chapter 2. At other times this loneliness is rooted in long-standing pain and hurt. In such situations, the experience of loneliness is calling the person to emotional growth. The emotionally empty person must first become more self-sustaining. Loneliness is calling for self-involvement before other-involvement can be satisfying.

This is indeed a paradoxical response. It may not seem to make much sense to suggest that some lonely persons need to focus more on themselves. However, it is a false expectation to believe that others can take away my inner loneliness. Henri Nouwen stated well his concern for those who are desperate for companions. He observed that frequently we are "driving ourselves into excruciating relationships, tiring friendships and suffocating embraces."[18] When you feel such drivenness, you need to attend more to your own emotional needs.

Loneliness associated with grief, depression, or physical illness may remind us of changed relationships. It is then time to attend to those relationships. Emotional growth depends upon relationship awareness. The experience of becoming deeply aware of the pains and joys of relationships is no small task. In grief, for example, we may learn more about what we truly valued in the lost relationship. To learn how to imagine our loved one's presence at crucial times may provide comfort. But we may also see how the relationship restricted our growth and limited our possibilities. Because of grief, we then become more able to experience the depth of our life movements.

But the pain of such relationships may also remind you of your inner emptiness. A realistic appraisal of your strengths and weaknesses in relationships may be distressing. At times this level of reflection and growth may be too frightening or painful for you to handle by yourself. A counseling relationship may both stimulate and support growth and development. To deepen your relationship awareness may demand a very intensive individual search. This paradoxical truth allows movement from pain to nurture. Sometimes your pain will need the nurture of a caring professional if you are to face your loneliness with courage and creativity.

Aloneness.—A key strategy which is often overlooked in facing emotional loneliness is increasing one's aloneness. When one chooses aloneness, there is space created for solitude. Solitude is "a paradoxical state of being alone and yet not alone."[19] Solitude allows me space to focus on my relationships with others and with God. In contrast to loneliness, solitude is a freeing, pleasant, and timeless experience. In this experience, the person discovers that he or she is not alone. Solitude can provide the bridge to companionship.

Solitude as a response to loneliness recognizes a basic relational principle. How I perceive myself and relationships is usually more important than what "really" is. By creating aloneness, you give yourself an opportunity to more carefully evaluate your own needs, to value the relationships which are available to you, and to allow God's presence to be known. If I believe myself to be unworthy and friendless, I will feel that way, even though my boss gives me a raise and my friends give me a surprise birthday party. Emotional nurture depends upon realizing that I have relationships to self, others, and God. This is true regardless of what my present pain may tell me. At this level, solitude makes space so that we can discover that we are not alone.[20]

Our need for solitude may mean *creating* alone time in order to have space for reflection. Job asked for such space during his suffering "Let me alone, that I may find . . . comfort" (Job 10:20). The psalmist was likewise aware that those who suffer may find special care in solitude: "God gives the desolate a home to dwell in" (Ps. 68:6). If you have the courage to create more aloneness, you may find an improvement in your relationships with self and others. In chapter

5, I will explore more fully how solitude may deepen our relationship with God.

One Woman's Journey

A young woman, Margaret, entered counseling because of her sense of worthlessness. She had experienced deep loneliness, profound depression including suicidal thoughts, and failed marriages. Her history illustrates personal experiences which may lead to emotional emptiness. She was born to well-educated parents who were dedicated to their careers. Both her parents traveled frequently. When her father was home he spanked Margaret and her siblings daily. He thought it was an expression of love. Her mother demanded perfection in school and home activities. She thought it was an expression of love. During childhood, Margaret's father died suddenly from heart disease. She blamed herself for his death since she had frequently wished him dead. Her mother quickly remarried only to discover that the man was abusive to both her and Margaret. A divorce quickly followed but not before Margaret had been badly hurt. As an adolescent, Margaret was sexually promiscuous. "It was the one time I could get someone to hold me." She married young, became pregnant, and divorced her irresponsible young husband. As a middle-aged professional, Margaret reached the end of her rope. Though she was outwardly successful and had many friends, she felt miserable inside. She was still sexually promiscuous. She could not truly believe that anyone really cared for her.

Margaret tested her counselor's commitment by missing sessions and threatening to harm herself. She resisted both creative solitude activities and recommended group involvements. Over a long period of time she slowly grew in trust and hope. She learned to enjoy solitary walks in a nearby state park. She came to realize that others had been through similar experiences. She attended survivor-of-abuse groups and found support and nurture. Later her commitments to self and others led to deeper commitments to God. After a rather long journey, Margaret seldom experienced loneliness. When she did, she was well aware of how to face it creatively.

Not all such emotionally starved people will be able to experience the same transformation as Margaret. Some will not have the patience or resources. Others will not invest the energy required for such an endeavor. They will remain lonely. They will be lonely, whether alone or in a crowd. But change is possible. Those who invest in both short-term and long-term strategies for nurture will reap rich dividends of growth.

Loneliness is a response at both personal and situational levels. Pained emotions will lead some into loneliness, no matter what the outer circumstances. Others' outer circumstances are so overwhelming that their isolation makes even the strongest cringe with fear. This chapter has focused on the personal, emotional side of this balance. The following chapter will focus more on the social, situational side of the pain of loneliness.

Notes

1. Raymond Paloutzian and Craig Ellison, "Loneliness, Spiritual Well-Being, and the Quality of Life," *Loneliness: A Sourcebook of Current Theory, Research, and Therapy,* eds. Letitia Peplau and Daniel Perlman (New York: Wiley and Sons, 1982), p. 229.

2. Sandra Louchs, "Loneliness, Affect, and Self-Concept: Construct Validity of the Bradley Loneliness Scale," *Journal of Personality Assessment* 44 (1980), pp. 142-147. See also Mohammadreza Hojat, "Loneliness as a Function of Selected Personality Variables," *Journal of Clinical Psychology* 38 (1982), pp. 137-141.

3. See Robert S. Weiss, ed., *The Experience of Loneliness: Studies in Emotional and Social Isolation* (Cambridge: Mass.: MIT Press, 1973).

4. David G. Weeks, et al, "Relations Between Loneliness and Depression: a Structural Equation Analysis," *Journal of Personality and Social Psychology* 39 (1980), pp. 1238-1244.

5. Carin Rubenstein, et al, "Loneliness," *Human Nature* 2 (1979), pp. 58-65.

6. Helena Lopata, et al, "Loneliness: Antecedents and Coping Strategies in the Lives of Widows," *Loneliness*, pp. 310-326.

7. Melva Vandiver, "A Christmas Crisis," *Guideposts*, Dec. 1986, pp. 42-44.

8. Quoted by Letitia Peplau, et al, "Loneliness and Self-Evaluation," *Loneliness*, p. 135.

9. Frank Stagg, *Polarities in Man's Existence in Biblical Perspective* (Philadelphia: Westminster Press, 1973), pp. 76-83.

10. Robert Neale, "Loneliness: Depression, Grief and Alienation," in Robert Wicks, et al, *Clinical Handbook of Pastoral Counseling* (New York: Paulist Press, 1985), p. 469.

11. Herbert P. Leiderman, "Pathological Loneliness: a Psychodynamic Interpretation," *The Anatomy of Loneliness*, eds. Joseph Hartog, et al (New York: International Universities Press, 1980), pp. 377-393.

12. F. V. Wenz, "Seasonal Suicide Attempts and Forms of Loneliness," *Psychological Reports* 40 (1977), pp. 807-810.

13. James Lynch, *The Broken Heart: The Medical Consequences of Loneliness* (New York: Basic Books, 1979), p. 4.

14. Donald A. West, R. Kellner, and M. Moore-West, "The Effects of Loneliness: A Review of the Literature," *Comprehensive Psychiatry* 27 (1986), pp. 351-363.

15. H. T. Reis, et al, "On Specificity in the Impact of Social Participation on Physical and Psychological Health," *Journal of Personality and Social Psychology* 48 (1985), pp. 456-471.

16. R. M. Page, S. Wrye, and G. Cole, "The Role of Loneliness in Health and Wellness," *Home Healthcare Nurse* 4 (1986), pp. 6-10.

17. Stagg, *Polarities*, pp. 66-83.

18. Henri J. M. Nouwen, *Reaching Out* (Garden City, N.J.: Doubleday, 1975), p. 19.

19. Robert E. Neale, *Loneliness, Solitude, and Companionship* (Philadelphia: Westminster Press, 1984), p. 54.

20. Neale, *Loneliness*, p. 72.

4

Social Loneliness
and Community

"A threefold cord is not quickly broken" proclaimed the writer of wisdom (Eccl. 4:12). Those who live in relationship—"threefold"— are not easily broken. Relationships sustain us in difficult and frightening times.

"Young and Old Alike Can Lead Lonely Lives in New U.S. Suburbs" proclaimed a recent newspaper article.[1] The article told the stories of families who are participating in the "American dream." They have purchased new homes in fast-growing suburbs of exciting cities. However, instead of happiness they find isolation. They do not know neighbors, streets, history, or place. Their children long for their old friends. Both parents and children feel left out where there are "in groups" already established. They are as likely to move within three years as they are to remain in their dream house. "Shallow roots" lead to a sense of "nothing here makes sense."

Similar experiences of isolation occur when persons retire and move to "that spot in the sun." Old relationships, churches, and patterns of life disappear. Some may find it very difficult to reestablish roots. This may happen even with those who retire "to be closer to children." They find their children living in suburbs with other young families. The retired couple find little in common with the persons around them. Nostalgia, a longing for old ways of living, may dominate both thinking and feeling. Their isolation leads to loneliness.

But physical isolation is not the only type of isolation experienced in our culture. Broken marriages, substance abuse, family violence, and a lack of social skills are even more painful causes of isolation and loneliness. While physical isolation can sometimes be overcome through rather simple processes, other forms of isolation are more long lasting and damaging. The psalmist expressed this feeling with his cry: "I looked for pity . . . / and for comforters, but I found none" (Ps. 69:20). As the psalmist prayed for deliverance from his enemies, he realized his isolation and helplessness.

Isolation, violence, and lack of comforters are certainly contributors to the basic form of social loneliness from a biblical perspective. This loneliness is alienation. One who feels alienated feels different from those around him. He feels like a foreigner, as if he is among many people who have different values and speak different languages. Or she feels detached or broken off from belonging with and to others. Although alienation and loneliness are not always experienced together, they are certainly frequent companions. Scripture speaks of the pain of alienation from others and demonstrates its devastating consequences on individuals and communities.

A scriptural story of alienation.—In John 4 we read of Jesus' encounter with "The Woman at the Well." Jesus was resting at midday near a well while His disciples went into a village for food. They were traveling through Samaria. A woman approached the well and Jesus began to talk with her. This was one of the more remarkable and extended of Jesus' dialogues.

Jesus first offered the woman "living water" which she confused with flowing water. He then offered her water that would never leave her thirsty which she confused with actual physical water. He offered her the living God which she confused with a debate between the Jews and the Samaritans over how and where God was to be worshiped. Finally He confronted her deepest alienation: bring your husband here. She confessed that she had no husband to which Jesus responded with divine insight: you have had five husbands and the man you now live with is not our husband.

She lived in a remarkably immoral situation. There is little doubt that she was the community scandal. The woman's presence at noon at a public well was clear indication of her alienation. Their custom was for the women to gather in the early morning and the late evening to collect their household's water needs for that day. This woman was not welcome by her neighbors. She was excluded, detached, and broken off. Her multiple marriages may have been a significant factor in her not being welcome to join the other women. Her labor was solitary, hot, and lonely. The woman's encounter with Jesus had rather strange impact. She collected her community and brought them to meet Jesus. The one who was alienated was responsible for gathering others at the feet of Jesus. Perhaps she had been a victim of tragic circumstances. She knew well the fact that "victims always feel lonely."[2] In meeting Jesus, her alienation was overcome.

The impact of this story cannot be fully appreciated without noting its place in the Gospel of John. In John 3, there is an account of Jesus' evening meeting with Nicodemus. Nicodemus was a wealthy and well connected rabbi. On the outside he appeared to have no sense of alienation. Nevertheless, he went away from Jesus without creating a stir. Yet in John 4 we read of this poor, alienated Samaritan woman. She responded positively to Jesus' revelation and led others to him. This woman had to begin living her life responsibly and relationally with others. Perhaps she had been a victim. But she was no longer controlled by her past. The paradox between the wealthy, respected rabbi and the poor, despised woman cannot be overemphasized. Alienation comes in many forms. Only those willing to face their true condition will be given grace to live life in a new way.

American society.—A recent best-selling book *Habits of the Heart* reports several trends in American society which increase the danger of loneliness. One of these trends is the emphasis on "finding oneself."[3] Society stresses self-reliance, leaving home, and work as the centers of life. There are even forces which encourage persons to leave other groups such as churches. It is difficult for us to appropriately accept duty and authority from outside of self. There is little basis for a common vision of what constitutes virtue in living. We have little agreement on common guiding values. The authors recommend the antidote for such an emphasis is to stress participation, community, and commitment. They are convinced that persons need a transcendent call from a God who challenges, promises, and reassures.

A second force in American culture which drives us to loneliness is "individualism."[4] Individualism forms the center of American culture. Two of our favorite characters in books and on television have been the cowboy and the detective. Each of these represent autonomous individual striving. They also tell us to ignore personal danger, pain, and suffering for the good of a cause. Thus cowboys and detectives, our heroes, are frequently isolated persons. When they become our "romantic ideals," we strive to their same kind of individual performance. However, this isolation may become loneliness for many. In isolation, persons are more likely to be manipulated and driven to conformity. Individualism is a core value which has dangers. One central danger is that it may lead to loneliness.

This chapter will identify the pain of social isolation by examining specific situations of alienation. It will then suggest methods of coping with and changing this isolation. The pain of social isolation is rooted in our need for relationships. When loneliness results from social isolation and alienation, we need to focus our attention on relational issues. Emotional need and spiritual separation can also bring on loneliness. But in this chapter I am focusing on loneliness due to pain in relationships. Our relationships involve other individuals, groups of persons, and family generations. Relationships may also involve material possessions and the world of nature.

The Pain of Social Isolation

Social isolation is a familiar experience for most of us. It is more difficult to define in precise ways. Most of us will remember the summer when our best friend's family went on vacation and we had no one to play with for two weeks. We felt isolated. You may have said good-bye to spouse and children, traveled to a distant city, and conducted business for three weeks. During those three weeks there was no significant contact with others outside of business acquaintances. You felt isolated.

In a technical sense, social isolation refers to a lack of interactional networks such as kin, confidants, and friends. These relational networks serve functions such as talking, helping, and having fun. When we do not have sufficient persons with whom we can talk and have fun, we feel social isolation.

I must emphasize again that social isolation is not the same as loneliness. Nor is social isolation always detrimental. For example, while writing this book, I have spent many hours away from my normal network of family and friends. My isolation has given me space in which to be productive with this project. I have not felt lonely because I have not felt the drive to relationships. Social loneliness results when isolation, a felt need for companionship, and a lack of available companions are all present. Under these conditions, isolation leads to loneliness which is extremely painful.

Social isolation has both emotional and physical impact. I discussed the physical impact of emotional loneliness in chapter 3. Here I emphasize the physical impact of social loneliness. A study of two hundred men made after their college graduations focused on what life-style elements would lead to a longer physical life.[5] The key health factor was not exercise, diet, or type of work. Rather, the biggest difference in health depended on how extensive and intensive their relationships were. The more involved with others the men were, the healthier they were. The smaller their social network, the more likely they were to experience illness.

The elderly may be particularly vulnerable to the physical effects of isolation.[6] Studies have demonstrated that persons who do not have a confidant are much more likely to be depressed and dissatisfied with life than are those who do have a confidant. Another crucial element is that those who have had a close relationship, but then lose it, are at great risk for increased illness and emotional difficulty. Widows and the divorced are at great risk for social isolation, loneliness, and physical and emotional illnesses.

Social isolation is painful to all of us in physical, emotional, and spiritual ways. Both the human sciences and Scripture agree at this point.

Scriptural Principles

Genesis 2:18 says, "It is not good for the man to live alone" (GNB). While the passage applies directly to marital relationships, it is also true for our need of relationships in general. It is not good for us to live in isolation from others.

"The Preacher" of Ecclesiastes also clearly knew this human and divine truth many centuries ago. In Ecclesiastes 4:9-12 we find eternally relevant thoughts on the importance of friendship.

Two are better than one, because they have a good reward for their toil.
For if they fall, one will lift up his fellow; but woe to him who is alone
when he falls and has not another to lift him up. Again, if two lie
together, they are warm; but how can one be warm alone? And though
a man might prevail against one who is alone, two will withstand him.
A threefold cord is not quickly broken.

In the larger context of Ecclesiastes 4:1-12, the Preacher holds that misery, greed, and envy are the core conditions of human life. Our life of misery is mitigated only by companionship. Greed and envy are always enemies of friendship. The advantages of cooperation far outweigh any good that may come from rivalry. Warmth, comfort, and security are only available in friendly relationships. Friendship itself is substantial reward. Solidarity in work, play, and love is essential to human fulfillment.

The Preacher's final image is particularly important. "A threefold cord is not quickly broken." Two persons together can eliminate social isolation. Two are better than one. But three persons are better yet. Three designated a sense of completeness to the ancient Hebrew mind. With three persons present, a strong bond of community could be woven. This bond could provide for both emotional and social needs.

I believe it is important to understand the nature of persons which makes this connection between alienation and loneliness so direct. Scripture's response to this problem is clear. For example, in Romans 14:7-8, the apostle Paul summarized a core Christian confession. "None of us lives to himself, and none of us dies to himself. If we live, we live to the Lord, and if we die, we die to the Lord; so then, whether we live or whether we die, we are the Lord's." Faith in Jesus Christ allows God to overcome our alienation. Therefore, in Christ we are never alone, even in death. Signs of Christian community are also evidence of the overcoming of alienation. We know that such experiences as love, trust, acceptance, confession, and forgiveness mark the Christian's relational experiences. One way to understand our human problem is that we tend to live alienated, isolated, and broken lives. The gospel promise is that, in Christ, loneliness can be healed.

The Old Testament has an equally strong view of the importance of community in living a faithful life before God. The people of Israel viewed themselves as a whole with a "corporate personality."[7] This means that the community was responsible to each individual. What one person did affected the entire community. What the community chose was the choice for all. Individual rights and responsibilities were not their focus. The family or nation as a whole responded for all before God. There was an inseparable bond between individual and society.

For example, during Israel's journey from Egypt to the Promised Land, the people became impatient while their leader Moses was away on Mount Sinai. Some decided to make a calf of gold in order to worship. The entire people were punished as one for this sin of a few. Later Jewish writers such as Isaiah and Jeremiah saw more individual accountability before God. Yet they did not discard the principle that God's people are responsible as a whole for their entire membership. We are indeed part of a whole. Yet the individual maintains a separate identity and is accountable. Persons are created for community.

Our human nature demands that we live in community. Even though we do not think of ourselves as living with a "corporate personality," we do know the importance of healthy relationships for wholistic living.

Broken Relationships

The connection between isolation and changed relationships should be clear. Of course, change is inevitable. Change is usually painful, even though it may also be exciting and joyful. When our relationships change, pain is inevitable as well. The pain of changed relationships is frequently loneliness. When a person, an object, or a potential for a relationship has been lost, loneliness is likely to follow. The changes caused by moves, divorces, deaths, and other tragic situations are painful. But there is potential to overcome these experiences. New friends can be made. New levels of intimacy can be developed. Where there is pain there is also promise.

Our suffering from social isolation and relational brokenness is usually severe. However, when loneliness becomes a part of one's suffering, it becomes even more painful. Joan came to her pastor for help. Her chief complaint was, "I do not seem to have any friends." She was forty-four years old, had been twice divorced with no children, lived four hundred miles from her parents and siblings, and was ending a damaging relationship with a male friend. On top of all this, she had recently been moved by her company into a secretarial position in which she spent many hours each day with no companions nearby. Certainly there was much pain in her story. There were repeated failed attempts to relate with both men and women. But why had she chosen this time to ask for help? When asked this, her reply was, "I never needed relationships before like I need them now." At mid-life she was much more aware of her isolation, and she was taking stock of her brokenness. In that reevaluation period she was much more aware of her desire for caring relationships of all kinds. Her isolation and brokenness—her alienation—plus her desire for relationships had led to loneliness.

Our understanding of alienation can be deepened by examining several types of broken relationships which result in loneliness. Some of these may even be caused by loneliness at times. Problems of pained marriages, family violence, substance abuse, and poor social skills haunt many people. The problems lead to isolation, brokenness, and alienation. Loneliness may be a way of life for many people caught in the web of these human problems. I will emphasize the role of loneliness in these problems and ways to deal with the pain of loneliness in each. More than loneliness is usually painful in each of these areas, but loneliness will be our focus.

Pained Marriages

Bonnie tells a story familiar to many.[8] She tells of her difficulty keeping in touch with her spouse when the pressures of work, unexpected bills, and parenting children combined in the natural course of their life together. Bonnie tells of her older children asking, "What's wrong, Mom?" She tells of deep loneliness and separation from her husband. One day, after a particularly difficult morning, she happened to meet her pastor's wife in the grocery. Her friend's half-joking question, "What's the matter? Lose your best friend?" opened her load of pain. As she talked further with her friend later that day, Bonnie realized that she was responsible for some of her family's distance and separation. Her friend gave her little advice. But Bonnie heard what was crucial, "One of you has to take a risk and insist on communication and changes."

Bonnie developed a plan to go away for a weekend with her husband. This seemed like a really silly idea to her. They did not have the money. She was not certain he would want to be with her. She was not sure she wanted a weekend with this stranger. Yet she developed the plan, made arrangements for their children, withdrew their last money from their account, packed his bags, and "kidnapped him" after work. They spent the weekend talking, praying, watching movies, laughing, and dealing with painful issues. After returning home they still found it a challenge to talk. Sometimes it seemed easier just to keep their worries to themselves. They discovered that loneliness is not overcome by meeting another halfway. Sometimes one must go the whole distance in inviting healing into a pained marriage.

Husbands and wives become isolated. They fail to sit at the table for a few minutes to talk about the day. They do not make time to plan for an evening out, a weekend trip, or a family vacation. They slowly stop touching each other in sympathy and in romance. Pain grows, usually outside their awareness. One day, "out of nowhere," a crisis erupts. She becomes physically or emotionally ill. He leaves home after an angry argument. A sexual affair becomes known. The isolation and brokenness of their marriage pushes both into a very lonely condition.

Sometimes pained marriages are so disruptive and abusive to one or both partners that outsiders wonder what keeps the two people together. Others would assume that living without the pained marriage would be easier than fixing the marriage or staying in it. However, fear of loneliness is a major factor in convincing the two to stay with each other. Even when two people have very supportive relationships outside the marriage, they fear the loss of the one whom they have loved. Even when that love has turned to hate and bitterness, their fear of loneliness will drive persons to stay together. When another person is so important to me that I invest passionate love or passionate hate, I will fear loneliness if the loss of that relationship is threatened. Because we are created with such powerful needs for relationship, many will tolerate much pain before considering severing the relationship. Because change is so threatening, many will tolerate great pain before risking change.

In some pained marriages the partners fear that discussion of their concerns and problems will drive the other person away. They then try to keep their anxieties and stresses private. But that privacy creates the very problems they were attempting to avoid. When one person tries to keep thoughts and feelings away from another, distance and suspicion creep into the relationship. Worries grow that trust and hope are not being shared, thus someone else must be hearing about them. When a marriage becomes closed to discussion, deep pain is close at hand. Pastors and marriage counselors should be consulted very quickly.

In such situations, we should never underestimate the risk involved in openly discussing thoughts and feelings. To share oneself in this way is to risk being rejected. To open oneself for understanding is also to open oneself for rejection. Thus, loneliness can be allowed to fill the empty places of isolation and alienation. Resentments grow when unfinished arguments and broken promises are allowed to go undiscussed and unchallenged. A sense of being unappreciated and misunderstood grows when my unique characteristics and dreams are ignored. Blaming of my inner hurts and failures on spouse and child results in dumping emotions and thoughts in hurtful and damaging ways.

The pressures of life have a way of separating marital partners and their children from each other. A young professional couple with their two school-age children recently sat in my office. Their chief complaint was, "We don't know each other." As I listened to their stories, I believed they had diagnosed their problem exactly. However, helping them remedy the situation was difficult because they did not want to accept the necessary changes. Both parents were working ten-hour days. The children were carried by caretakers to a variety of dance, music, and sports lessons and events. In spite of all their work, their financial commitments took every extra penny they could earn. They were isolated from each other and the family was seriously broken. In spite of their pain and a clear understanding of the dangerous life-style they were living, they were unwilling to face their resentments and confront their misunderstandings. Isolation was building, and loneliness was a predictable result.

Pained marriages are a troubling source of loneliness. Whether the pain leads to divorce and thus separation or whether the pain stays within a "together" marriage, loneliness is an ever-present danger.

Violence at Home and in Society

We are told that American society is one of the most violent of any country on earth. We have very high rates of assault, murder, rape, and robbery. Sexual-abuse crimes within families and against non-family members occur at a high rate and are increasing at an alarming pace. Individuals and families who are impoverished and perhaps homeless are particularly liable to be caught in this vicious web. Can these frightening problems be related to loneliness? To some extent the answer is yes.

Child abuse.—The few studies on the relationship of loneliness and the violence of child abuse which are available indicate a reason for concern.[9] Neglectful mothers are more lonely than nonneglectful mothers. Isolation and loneliness are more likely present in abusing parents than in nonabusing parents. We cannot determine a cause for this relationship. For example, we do not know whether loneliness precedes child abuse or whether those who have abused children tend to isolate themselves from others. Whatever the exact relationship, however, it is clear that child abuse and loneliness go together.

We also know that those who suffered abuse and violence as children are more likely to abuse children later in life. Many grew up in deprived homes in which there was little opportunity for building trust. Later they were denied friendships due to their shame or frequent moves. Abusing parents tend to be more rigid and authoritarian than nonabusing parents. Their levels of stress also tend to be much higher. They tend to feel less need for friendships. They also have little emotional or cognitive understanding of ways to nurture children.

Abused children are frequently physically isolated. They are usually emotionally empty. They internalize their abuse as a sure indication of their worthlessness. They think, "My parents would not do this to me if I were not so bad!" Thus, violence in the parents leads to lonely children who are then more likely to be violent toward their own children. A pattern of abuse across several generations is not at all unusual.

This lack of empathetic concern was made particularly clear to me when I was asked to counsel Ann. Ann was a thirty-three-year-old woman, twice divorced, with a son ten years old. She had grown up in a middle-class home. Ann had completed both college and a professional school. She came for counseling complaining of poor self-esteem, failure in relationships, a sense of inadequacy as a parent, and overwhelming recurring nightmares. She told me in our first conversation that she had been abused as a child, but she told it without feeling. She denied remembering any details of the assaults. As we discussed her life it became evident that her father had spanked her on her bare bottom every day for no particular reason. This continued until he died suddenly when she was ten. Everyone in her family knew this, but she had never told anyone outside the family. She was totally alone in this experience.

As we continued our counseling relationship, Ann's nightmares became worse. Suddenly she realized that the nightmares were an actual event. Her mother had remarried when Ann was twelve. Her stepfather had sexually assaulted her in terribly violent ways. But no one had ever noticed. She had never told a single person. The emotional turmoil which engulfed Ann as she became aware of her violent heritage was tremendous. She was indeed a deeply pained and lonely woman. But she walked through the fires both in individual therapy and in adult-survivor-of-child-abuse groups. She came to understand why she had lived her life in such isolated and ineffective ways. As she came to terms with her heritage, both her emotional and her social loneliness were lifted. She became a more effective mother and more successful in her career.

Child abuse is closely associated with loneliness. Those who are the victims tend to live very lonely lives. Those who are the victimizers are also terribly isolated. Enabling the victims and victimizers to experience community is one key to reconciliation of their deep alienation.

The homeless.—The violence of poverty and homelessness which many families face is also associated with loneliness. It is difficult for those of us with some sense of financial security to appreciate the desperate conditions that so many persons live in. A recent news article summarized their plight well as it relates to social isolation.

> To say that the homeless need housing is a bit like saying the poor need money—both statements are true, but neither ultimately does

much to illuminate the problem. What's now clear is that if every homeless person were put in an affordable low-income apartment tomorrow, many would be back on the street several weeks later. The reason, as study after study has shown, is that the homeless are different from other poor people in one crucial respect: They are profoundly alone.

Whether they are single mothers on welfare or drug addicts, the homeless almost invariably lack friends, close ties with family members and any affiliation with a church or local organization. And for the homeless, that isolation typically transforms temporary crises, such as an apartment eviction or an alcoholic binge, into prolonged emergencies.[10]

The homeless reflect some of the deepest threads of violence, isolation, and loneliness at work in our society. Any serious help for the homeless will focus primarily on building a dependable social network. Their profound aloneness will be the focus of responses by individuals, churches, and society. Otherwise any response will be nothing more than a Band-Aid placed on a gushing wound.

Substance Abuse

By this point you are probably convinced that loneliness is a powerful condition which we will do almost anything to avoid. One self-destructive activity in which some engage in order to avoid the pain of their loneliness is substance abuse. Substance abuse refers to the use of alcohol and nonmedical drugs in addictive and nonlegal ways. Substance abuse has many causes. Loneliness is one of the causes and one of the effects.

One study has reported that persons who attempt to avoid loneliness are more likely to use hard drugs than those who are willing to confront this painful situation. Other studies have attempted to evaluate the relationship between alcoholism and loneliness, but with inconclusive results.[11]

In chapter 3 I discussed the manner in which an illness may result in separation from loved ones thereby leading to loneliness. The substance abuser has the additional burden that the illness itself may well have alienated his support system. Parents, spouses, and friends may well have given up on the "hopeless drunk." Treatment is even more difficult without an active support system.

Loneliness also serves as an indicator of the quality of life of the substance abuser. The more loneliness is experienced, the poorer one's quality of life is likely to be. The poorer the quality of life, the more difficult the process of treatment and rehabilitation will be. Thus, substance abuse may be an attempt to avoid the pain of loneliness. Loneliness may make recovery from abuse even more difficult. This is another example of the vicious cycle which loneliness engenders in relationships.

Lack of Social Skills

Loneliness may also occur when a person has failed to learn basic social skills. Broken relationships result when one person or all people involved in the relationship do not possess the core skills of human relating. In writing about basic social skills I am thinking of such core values as interest in another's feelings and thoughts, simple courtesy, responsive conversation, and attending to the needs of others. Some lonely people lack the skills necessary to engage in effective social interaction. These social deficits may be present at both individual and group levels of interaction.

Studies have demonstrated that persons who experience the death of a parent at an early age have much greater likelihood of experiencing loneliness and depression later in life. They experience all relationships as unclear and uncertain. They may feel very hesitant about ever committing themselves deeply enough to a relationship to relieve their feelings of loneliness. Some are shy or seem distant to others and thus do not appear open to social involvement. Thus, they are never invited to become a part of "the group." Some people may appear "strange." Their "strangeness" may have resulted from parents who ignored them, overprotected them, or gave them mixed signals on how they should behave. All of these persons have deficiencies which cause them to long for deep individual relationships. Yet their social deficits block them from ever achieving their goal.

At other times a person's ability to function in social settings may have been disrupted. Such disruptions occur for many reasons. Some people do not experience "good-enough" parenting as a child and thus never develop a sense of empathy for others. Others fail to develop relationships as a school child and adolescent and thus never develop the capacity to carry on a conversation. Others experience some tragedy such as illness or accident. They may be isolated or physically disfigured to such an extent that normal relationships become very difficult for them to bear. Each of these situations create long-term relational handicaps.

Persons with such relational deficits are often characterized by negativism, rejecting attitudes, self-absorbed thoughts, self-deprecating feelings, and low responsiveness to others.[12] When presented with an opportunity their first response is no! They tend to discount and devalue others' ideas, accomplishments, and feelings. They find it very difficult to extend themselves beyond their own inner worlds. They feel bad about their own abilities, dreams, and possibilities. They are not able to indicate any interest in others' plans and proposals. One television character who personified such traits was Dr. Frank Burns on "M.A.S.H." He could never see any value in others' thoughts, plans, or ways of living. Clearly, such an individual experiences social isolation and is vulnerable to loneliness.

If you have suffered broken relationships because of a lack of social skills you will probably recognize the following experiences. When in a large group of people, you may feel "by myself." You may have an inner sense that you are somehow different from others. There are times when you feel like you do not even know yourself. The danger of such a situation is that desperate attempts to flee loneliness may follow. Some become "clowns" in social situations in order to feel a part of the group. Others "grease the tongue" with alcohol. Still others participate in promiscuous sex because they know no other way of relating. A deficit of social skills can lead to personal and social bankruptcy just as a deficit of money can lead to financial bankruptcy.

A lack of social skills can also inhibit relationships with larger groups thereby leaving one feeling lonely. American society offers many opportunities for social mobility, for voluntary association, and for physical moves. Socially skilled people may find it difficult to comprehend that some individuals cannot find a group with whom they feel comfortable. There is even a myth among church people that "Anyone can feel at home in our church." However, this very multitude of choices immobilizes some persons. The lonely may feel immobilized to choose a church to attend, which neighborhood to move to, what political organization to commit time and money to. The great number of choices leave some adrift, uncommitted, and lonely. Some lack the personal skills to deal effectively with the burden of such freedom.

The person who is lonely because of lack of individual relationship skills may experience feelings similar to the small child who lost her mother in the grocery. She felt panic and fear. The store shelves were *so high,* the aisles were *so long,* and the passing adults were *so tall.* She felt an overwhelming emptiness and desolation. She could not imagine ever finding her mother again. Tears and hysteria flowed. She was totally overcome. The first step in developing the skills required to relate interpersonally is to learn to cope with such overpowering feelings.

The person who is lonely because of a lack of group relationship skills may experience other feelings. A sense of boredom and aimlessness may reign. This is more like the school-age child who seldom sees his friends during summer vacation and complains, "I have nothing to do." He could ride his bike, walk to the park, read a book, or call a friend. But he complains instead. The first step required to cope with this deficit is to learn to take a risk in response to others.

A Reprise

These paragraphs on broken relationships may have been painful for you to read. They were certainly painful for me to write. Each of us have experienced enough occasions of social brokenness that we recall our pain. Even the healthiest marriage suffers from seasons of distance and aloneness. Almost no family is free from the pain of alcohol and substance abuse. Violence in home and society is a frightening prospect. All of us have felt uncomfortable in certain situations because our skills were not a match for what we had to face. However, those who face these experiences daily are too well aware of their depth of pain. The lonely are truly broken in these areas of life.

The following section will focus on ways the socially isolated can confront their loneliness. Changes in attitudes and development of skills are both required.

The Promise of Community

The pain of social isolation can be met by the presence of community. This may seem rather simplistic. Am I saying anything more than "If you do not have relationships, then go make some?" I certainly am. I am well aware that it is no small feat for socially isolated persons to develop a pleasing balance of community and aloneness. Companionship and aloneness are essential components in a healthy community. The socially lonely long for a life-style through which they can keep in touch with other people and group events.

A Biblical Perspective

Jesus' words in John 15 may provide the best biblical model of how we are to face social isolation and alienation. This chapter is part of Jesus' last words to His disciples before His betrayal. In this chapter, Jesus described the relationships which characterize a believer's life. Jesus first described the relationship between Him and His followers as like that of a grape vine and its branches. A first step in overcoming loneliness is to be a part of Christ.

Jesus was clear that we demonstrate our unity with Him by prayer and obedience to his Commandments. His commandment was "love one another" (John 13:34; 15:17). Our commitment to Jesus calls for us to love others. This is the second step in overcoming loneliness—to risk our own fears on behalf of others.

In John 15:18-27, Jesus instructed us in the third step for living a Christian social life. He warned us that the believer's relationship to others will sometimes bear the marks of misunderstanding and difficulty. Some persons in this world will not understand or accept us. This is true regardless of how well we learn to relate to others. I will use these three steps as a guide in discussing how social loneliness can be faced.

Abiding in Christ.—Those who experience social loneliness will frequently believe that there is no one who cares about them or for them. Their sense of isolation may be overwhelming. It is important for Christians to remember first that we are never absolutely alone. Jesus knew that he was never alone: "Yet I am not alone, for the Father is with me" (John 16:32). Since the Holy Spirit, the Comforter, is always present with the Christian, we too can make the same claim: I am not alone, for God is with me.

This affirmation is not intended to trivialize a lonely person's pain. Nor is it intended to offer an easy answer to a very difficult problem. It is necessary, however, to set the appropriate context for relationships. Those who feel estranged, alienated, and lonely certainly need human companionship. They need someone to hear them. Wayne Oates has written to this point well.

> You will find at the core of countless numbers of individuals an estrangement, a loneliness, a feeling on their part that no one cares for their soul, and a querulous sense of strangeness that anyone would genuinely take the time to listen and understand them.[13]

The lonely frequently need a listening human ear to remind them of God's compassion.

The truth must be maintained, however, that our human ears are but pale imitations of God's great compassion for us. Those who suffer from an absence of satisfying human relationships may also suffer from an absence of feeling God's presence. Chapter 5 will more fully explore this problem of spiritual loneliness. Here I will simply and directly say that the socially deprived lonely may find benefit in increasing their times alone. These alone times can be used to allow communion with God. Solitude with God is not just idle time. It may involve activities such as enjoying God's creation through walks in a forest or watching a sunset over the ocean. It may involve intensive study of Scripture. It may involve meditation and prayer in various forms.

The result of solitude with God can be dramatic. The importance placed on social deficiencies may be dramatically reduced. One's sense of living in a world of relationships and love may be increased. Sometimes the relational blocks which kept one from creative living are confronted in such times of solitude. These confrontations allow freedom to emerge as God brings healing. Communion with God is an essential backdrop for improving relational skills.

Love one another.—The next arena of growth for the socially lonely is more direct. The question is usually asked something like

"With whom and in what ways can I be a friend?" "How can I change my relationships so that I have friends?"

The first step in friendship is to evaluate the friendships you already have. There are many levels of friendship.[14] You may find it helpful to take pen and paper, write the categories which I will describe across the top of the page, and list persons under each category which fit that kind of friendship.

"Convenience friends" are those with whom I routinely interact. They include people such as neighbors and work companions. We should not place too high expectations upon these friends for intimacy and closeness. We can hope for common courtesy and perhaps even occasional conversations about matters of mutual interest. We cannot build our worlds around these friends.

"Special-interest friends" are those with whom we have a concern in common. These interests can include such things as sports, social and community-action programs, and certain work partners. These are members of our softball team or people who volunteer with us to teach a children's Sunday School class. At work these would be the people we extensively discuss common problems or projects. We can talk readily and deeply about the interests we share. We should not expect these friendships to go beyond this area. On occasion, a special-interest friendship can be broadened into a deeper relationship.

"Historical friends" are those people from the past who were once close to us. We are likely to enjoy reminiscing with them. They are important because they add a sense of history to our daily lives. They help us remember where we have been, our goals and dreams, and our deeper emotional and cultural roots. They can help us keep a perspective on our current situation, especially if our life journey has meant large moves, either geographically or socially. High-school or college class reunions may be times when we reconnect with these historical friends. The danger of these friends is that we can get trapped in nostalgia, the feeling of "the good old days." The days in which we did feel socially connected may lead to more pain than joy because of our present situation. Nevertheless, these friends offer potent resources for friendship.

"Crossroads friends" are those who have shared a crucial intersection in our life. These intersections were usually a time of crisis or life change. These are people who were not very important to us prior to some crucial event and may not have been very close after the event. But at the moment of crisis they were there for us. For example, I recall a college friend who was very helpful to me during the time I was deciding to enter pastoral ministry. I have had very little contact with him since that time, but I will always recall his love with thankfulness.

"Cross-generational friends" are those persons of different generations than our own with whom we have been mutually encouraging. We have learned from each other despite, or maybe even because of, our difference in age. I have watched my daughter enjoy such a friendship with one of my aunts. My daughter has learned several crafts from this aunt. She has also responded with warmth to my aunt's stories about her own childhood. On the other hand, I believe my aunt has found encouragement and energy through my daughter's curiosity and evident love.

"Close friends" are those with whom we emotionally and physically maintain ongoing communication. It is these friends that the socially isolated have the most difficulty developing. Close friends are those we consider to be companions. We tend to plan activities and share dreams. We share a sense of empathy, of feeling the joy and pain of the other. Close friends can be called upon for the most important events and the most insignificant trivia of life. Friendship at this level does not demand constant, or even frequent, communication. But when close friends do communicate, they do so with much interest and investment.

Each of these levels of friendship is important. To "love one another" calls for a balanced network of friendship. We should not expect a person at one level of friendship to be closer and more intimate than is appropriate to the relationship. Friendships depend on a balance between togetherness and solitude in these relationships.

Expect difficulty.—Jesus' message in John 15 also includes the message that we should expect difficulties in our relationships. Of course, the focus of Jesus' message was on the persecution that believers could expect from unbelievers. But the truth also applies to friendship patterns. One myth of marriage is: "and they lived happily ever after." The truth is that marriages and friendships are full of disappointment and difficulty. Some who are socially lonely believe that since they cannot develop a perfectly satisfying relationship, they must not have any friendships. That is not true.

Even the best relationships will suffer through difficult times. In Acts we read of the apostle Paul's first missionary journey. Barnabas was his trusted and close companion. Later, they came to a serious disagreement over another companion for the second journey. They had such a fight that Paul went one way and Barnabas another (Acts 15:36-41). There is no evidence that they ever reconciled their differences. However, later Paul did affirm Barnabas as an apostle of Christ (1 Cor. 9:6). No one has perfect friendships throughout life.

During difficult times in a friendship, specific steps should be taken to reconcile differences. The first step will usually be to overcome the fears which paralyze us from taking the risk of reaching out to others who have hurt us. Prayer and support from other friends may help overcome these fears.

The model for reconciliation found in Matthew 18:15-18 then offers clear steps to take. First, talk directly with the person with whom you have the difficulty. Be ready to clearly take responsibility for your part of the conflict. Expect them to take responsibility for their share. If that does not resolve the conflict, you may take two or three trusted friends into your confidence. Express your concerns to them and go talk with your friend. Be ready to change your own thoughts and behavior where necessary. If these steps are unsuccessful you may wish to talk with your pastor or spiritual leader. They may be able to provide guidance or act as a mediator in your conflict. If these steps do not resolve your difficulty, you and your friend may need to say good-bye to each other. This will certainly produce grief, but it will also give you freedom to begin new relationships.

Interpersonal Relationship Skills

There are specific skills which may be learned and practiced by those who are socially isolated and yearn for more satisfying relationships. Some persons need to commit themselves to specific activities in order to change their social patterns and networks. The socially isolated woman who works in a one-secretary office, goes directly home every evening, goes nowhere other than the grocery on Saturday, and watches church services and old movies on television all day Sunday is likely to continue feeling lonely. Certain skills and behavior patterns must be learned and practiced.

Essential skills.—Companionship does require communication and relational skills. These skills seem to be easy for some people to use while others struggle to carry on a simple conversation. Essential skills include active listening and self-disclosure.

Active listening refers to the responses a listener can make to develop empathy, closeness, and clarity with another person. Thomas Gordon, a popular writer, describes these behaviors in detail in *Parent Effectiveness Training* and in *Teacher Effectiveness Training*. His book for parents is applicable to all persons, whether they are parents are not. Behaviors of active listening start with the very simple nonverbal behaviors. In a conversation it is important to maintain eye contact. This does not mean that two people must stare holes through each other. But it does mean that frequent eye contact should be made. In a similar way the listener's posture should indicate attention to and concern for the person.

Active listening also includes simple verbal responses. Questions which are asked should be opening rather than closing. For example, questions which can be responded to with a yes or no generally do not open conversation. When I am listening to another, I will also want to be careful not to switch topics. When my aim is to express my interest in the other person, it is important that I respond to their *feelings* as well as their ideas. If something they say seems to invite happiness or sadness, I can respond with "Oh, you really sound happy about that," or, "That event must have been very painful." These responses indicate I am hearing and understanding my friend's ideas and feelings.

Active listening also demands that I show respect for the other person. If I am to develop a friendship, I must communicate regard and caring. If I wish to be cared for as a person of worth, I will respond to the value and worth of others. Most people will treasure friends who clearly affirm their value to them. We all need the boost of knowing that another person really cares about our welfare. We enjoy those who can affirm us, accept our good and bad points, and appreciate our uniqueness. Active listening skills enable us to demonstrate this care.

Friendships Follow

A second relational skill necessary to friendship is self-disclosure. Friendships require that I be a good speaker. This does not mean that I must be able to be eloquent or deep, either publicly or privately. It does mean that I need skills in communicating my thoughts and feelings. Self-disclosure begins with being aware of my own inner reactions, feelings, and thoughts. This is another paradox of loneliness. The first step in being a friend is to become a better friend to myself. Many who are lonely do not listen to their own feelings and reactions. Because of this, they cannot express these feelings to others. Thus, their companions cannot feel close to them. Successful communication depends upon my identifying my inner reactions.

Self-disclosure also means expressing my feelings and thoughts to others. This begins with an inner commitment to change the private ways in which you have previously lived your life. Without the commitment to be more open, changed behavior will not follow. Conquering your fear is no easy step. But a resolution to develop a friendship with at least one other person with whom you can make genuine contact is an essential starting point.

Active listening and self-disclosure are core steps toward overcoming social isolation. You will find self-help books in your book store for further help in understanding these processes. Various groups in your community will also provide training in communication skills, assertiveness skills, and related subjects. Churches, school or community education projects, YMCA, and YWCA are good places to call for information. Some socially isolated persons will be so frightened or discouraged at the prospect of beginning this journey that further help will be needed. Some counselors have special interests and skills in helping persons with these problems. Frequently they will recommend involvement in group therapy as a way to confront and resolve these fears. You may ask your pastor or a trusted friend for further information about these available resources.

Behavioral patterns.—Companionship also requires certain patterns of behavior. For the socially isolated person to make life-style changes which allow friendships to develop is not easy. Yet life-style changes will have to be made if the socially isolated person is to develop companions.

The first step in changing your behavioral patterns is to evaluate your present relationship network. Who are your friends? What kind of friend do you want to have? Our preceding discussion of the levels of friendships should provide some clues as to where you need to emphasize changes. Bob may have many "special-interest friends" and yet no "close friends." He feels lonely. Susan may have two "close friends" but no "special-interest friends." She, too, feels lonely. This man and woman will need very different strategies if they are to overcome their isolation.

The primary strategy for those who want to develop "close friends" is to increase the frequency and quality of contacts with those people. Bob will need to identify two or three persons with whom he senses similar interests. He will then make opportunities to be with them. If he is so isolated that he has no ideas about whom he would like to have as friends, Bob will need to first involve himself with others. He will need to go out of his way to meet his neighbors. He will need to participate in small groups such as Sunday School classes, hobby clubs, sports groups, and volunteer service organizations. Once Bob has made contacts with persons and identified those who might be close friends, he will need to consistently practice the relational skills of listening and self-disclosure.

Susan's strategies to lessen her isolation will be somewhat different. Since she has close friends already, she must have fairly good relational skills. Her first task is to broaden her circle on contacts. She will need to make time for games, volunteer activities, and small groups of people with similar interests. She may become active in her children's parent-teacher organization. She may volunteer to serve on the missions committee for her church's women's group. She may take classes at the YWCA or community education center. Any of these activities would broaden her circle of friends.

Once you have assessed your needs and made a strategy for meeting those needs, the next step for changing behavior comes into focus. Develop your willingness to take a risk! This is frequently the most difficult step of all. Studies have shown that one of the primary behavioral characteristics of the lonely is less willingness to take a risk.[15] A rather painful cycle is then set up in which the isolated person h is few companions, fails to develop social skills, anticipates rejection and isolation, feels rejected, and has fewer companions. Those who have been socially inactive usually find great difficulty in stepping outside their safe, if lonely, cocoon. To break this cycle requires courage.

A final step in making behavioral changes is to develop patience. Those who have been isolated for much or most of their lives should not expect to immediately become "party animals." Most will not go from being inactive in politics to a seat on the school board in eight months. Most will not go from being inactive in church to serving as chair of the personnel committee in six months. Most will not go from having no close friends to being overwhelmed with intimacy in three months. Breaking old life-style patterns is hard. It is frequently slow and full of setbacks. Those who expect alienation must shift both attitudes and behavior if companionship is to emerge.

Conclusion

Social isolation is a frightening experience. Isolation, alienation, and loneliness damage individual self-esteem and limit society's care for "the least of these." Physical illness, broken marriages, and violence in many forms are closely associated with loneliness.

However, there are possible courses of action which the lonely can take. These courses require courage and patience. Neither of these virtues is easy to develop. For those with a willingness to face their problems and take small, consistent steps toward their goals, social isolation will be reduced. Community will conquer loneliness.

Notes

1. Betsy Morris, "Young and Old Alike Can Lead Lonely Lives in New U.S. Suburbs," *The Wall Street Journal,* 27 Mar. 1987, p. 1.

2. Ira J. Tanner, *Loneliness: The Fear of Love* (New York: Harper and Row, 1973), p. 80.

3. Robert N. Bellah, et al, *Habits of the Heart: Individualism and Commitment in American Life,* (Berkeley: University of California Press, 1986), pp. 55-84.

4. Bellah, *Habits of the Heart,* pp. 142-163.

5. Richard C. Meyer, "Helping the 'Alone' Not to be Lonely," *Faith At Work,* (Nov. 1986), p. 11.

6. James A. Thorson and Bruce J. Horacek, "Self-Esteem, Value, and Identity," *Journal of Religion and Aging* 3 (Fall/Winter 1986), pp. 5-16.

7. H. Wheeler Robinson, *The Christian Doctrine of Man,* 2nd ed. (London: T. and T. Clark, 1913), pp. 27-30.

8. Bonnie G. Wheeler, "Keeping in Touch," *Guideposts,* Aug. 1987, pp. 38-41.

9. D. A. West, R. Kellner, and M. Moore-West, "The Effects of Loneliness: A Review of the Literature," *Comprehensive Psychiatry,* 27 (1986), p. 356.

10. "The Homeless," *U.S. News and World Report,* 29 Feb. 1988, p. 27.

11. West, et al, "The Effects of Loneliness," pp. 355-356.

12. Warren Jones, "Loneliness and Social Behavior," *Loneliness: A Sourcebook of Current Theory, Research, and Therapy,* eds. Letitia Peplau and Daniel Perlman (New York: Wiley and Sons, 1982), p. 249.

13. Wayne E. Oates, *The Christian Pastor,* 3rd ed. (Philadelphia: Westminster Press, 1982), p. 95.

14. Judith Viorst, *Necessary Losses* (New York: Simon and Schuster, 1986), pp. 179-180.

15. Norman Schultz, Jr., and Dewayne Moore, "Loneliness: Correlates, Attributions, and Coping Among Older Adults," *Personality and Social Psychology Bulletin,* 10 (1984), pp. 67-77.

5

Spiritual Loneliness and Solitude

James lived a "normal" busy life as businessman, father, husband, community volunteer, and church deacon. He was relatively successful in all of his ventures. He had many companions and a few close friends. However, one day James's family went on a brief weekend trip without him. He had to cancel the busy day of golf-and-yard work he had planned because it started raining. He was home, alone, with no plans. Suddenly a strange wave of emotion swept over him and left him deeply disturbed. This was something new that he had never experienced before. He tried to contact a couple of friends, but they were not home. Unable to contact friends or to do work, James had to face himself. He realized that he did not know himself. He knew that his many outward ventures had left him inwardly impoverished. He began to wonder how well he knew others. In that profound moment of honesty he reached an even deeper truth—he felt alone before God.

Over the next few weeks James resumed his regular busy life, but he could not forget the profound disturbance he had experienced. He finally consulted with his pastor who counseled with James. His counsel was creatively directed to helping James create more silent spaces in his life. In that process James found that he had been cutting off his awareness of his deep loneliness. He was also cutting off his need for God's presence to give life to his multitude of "good actions." Slowly James grew to develop his solitude, his aloneness with God.

While not everyone has quite as dramatic an experience of aloneness as did James, all of us either face or hide from the same awareness of our ultimate aloneness before God. In previous chapters we have considered loneliness which comes from within our broken selves and from our broken communities. There is yet another level of loneliness. It is well expressed in Augustine's thought, "Thou has made us for Thyself, and our hearts are restless until they find rest in Thee." This chapter will focus on loneliness which comes from our broken relationship with God.

The biblical account.—We should review the nature of our broken relationship with God. In Genesis 1 and 2 we read of the provisions which God made for our physical, emotional, relational, and spiritual welfare. Work, pleasure, companionship, and God's presence were all readily available. However, man and woman ate the fruit of the tree which gives knowledge of good and evil. Although they had all the provisions they needed for their welfare, they chose to act contrary to God's purpose for them. In their choice they separated themselves from God.

Genesis 3:8-13 records how man and woman became ashamed of their nakedness and hid from God in the garden. In their sin they knew separation from God. God's punishment was to cast them out of the garden. Their intimate, immediate relationship with God was broken. The careful provisions for their welfare were not totally eliminated. They still had what they needed for their physical, emotional, relational, and spiritual welfare. But now these were not immediately available. They had to work for their food. They suffered sadness, fear, and anger. There were arguments, jealousy, and murder. Their worship of God was distant and ritualistic. They experienced spiritual aloneness.

The curse laid upon Adam and Eve still is powerful today. However, we know that the ultimate victory has already been won through the life, death, and resurrection of Jesus Christ. "For as in Adam all die, so also in Christ shall all be made alive" (1 Cor. 15:22; see also

Rom. 5:12-21). Nevertheless, our relationship to God is often characterized by distance, pain, and hopelessness. We are ultimately cut off from God's presence in our humanity and thus do not have the spiritual resources necessary for wholeness. We are ultimately alone, separated from the God who is always there. God's work was climaxed in Jesus Christ and will be completed in God's future. In the meantime, we only partially know the victory and assurance of God's presence. Much of the time we know more of the pain of aloneness.

The Pain of Spiritual Aloneness

No matter how much we struggle to hide our true condition, one fact is always present. We are individuals before God. We are finally and ultimately alone. Loneliness is inescapable. We are separate from all other persons. We long for a community and hope to find meaningful and stimulating relationships. Finally, however, there is no escape from our aloneness. In all of creation, there is no one who fully and totally is in absolute harmony with me. For all of our good intentions, we remain separate. Our human pain and promise are rooted in and developed from this fact.

Loneliness is woven too deep within the fabric of life for it to be removed by individual effort or by intimate community. We are tempted to avoid this loneliness in a multitude of ways. But we must not push to solve problems of loneliness through individual busyness or through frantic friendship. If we do so, we will ignore our essential individuality before God. James, whom we met at the beginning of this chapter, did not truly allow God to be present until he could provide space, quiet, and solitude to meet God.

Jacob's Experience

The biblical story of Jacob teaches us this truth (see Gen. 32:22-32). Jacob had stolen his brother's birthright. A birthright was a special blessing for the oldest son from his father. Thus, Jacob was on the move; he was running from his brother. He was broken in self and broken from his community. But, he had not yet faced his central aloneness. In the course of his journey, he came to the banks of the brook Jabbok. There Jacob sent his family ahead while he remained alone. During the night he wrestled with the angel of the Lord. He did not wrestle with God's messenger when surrounded by family, but when he was alone. He did not wrestle during the bustle of his journey but in the quiet of the night. During this time of wrestling, Jacob was wounded. During his solitary wrestling with God he was scarred for life. In the pain of that wound, however, he received a blessing. That blessing was signified by a new name. His new name was "Israel": he who strives with God (Gen. 32:28). By that new name he moved from his essential aloneness before God, to knowing his place within God's plan. He was the one through whom God's rule and blessing would be shared with the world.

Like Jacob, we need to create times of solitude and aloneness. Our busy worlds need to come to a halt, so we can wrestle with God's meaning and purpose for us. We are ultimately alone because we are separated from God. In our times of aloneness and stillness we may allow God to be present.

Our Experiences

There are two life experiences which most powerfully illustrate our essential aloneness. In these experiences we flee solitude. These experiences are our feelings of guilt and our fear of death. How we face our guilt and how we deal with death are the essential tests of our relationship to God.

The pain of guilt.—Guilt results from my awareness that I have done some act which was wrong. I have failed. I cannot run away from that failure nor can I cover it up. No matter how hard I try, I cannot make someone else responsible for my failure. At that time each person stands naked before God. Guilt is a complex emotional and spiritual experience. We may respond to our failure with sadness, anger, denial, anxiety, rationalization, and a host of other responses. When Adam and Eve became aware of their wrongdoing, they hid from God.

Guilt is an experience of ultimate aloneness. When we are guilty, our loneliness exists as a form of judgment upon our guilt. At such times we realize the deep-seated apartness we feel from others and especially from God. We will do almost anything to escape the loneliness of guilt. Some try to give enough money to their favorite church or charity to try to assuage their guilt. They also hope to buy friends and the favor of a community. Others will suffer through intense unpleasurable experiences attempting to atone for their wrongdoing. They will go to great lengths to help others and to deny themselves fulfillment of their hopes and dreams. Our guilt feelings both indicate our aloneness and lead to further loneliness.

In 2 Samuel 11—12, we read of one man's experience of failure and guilt. King David saw the wife of an army officer who was fighting against Israel's enemies. He lusted for Bathsheba and made her pregnant. David attempted to cover up his deed by calling Uriah home. But Uriah would not see his wife because of his vows as a fighter in a holy war. David then sent Uriah to his death in an ill-advised attack. Later, David took Bathsheba as his wife. But David could not cover his guilt, nor his failure to live by God's moral standards. He was confronted by the prophet Nathan. At this point David confronted his guilt directly, confessed his sin to God, and received forgiveness. Psalm 51 may well have been written at this time.

> Have mercy on me, O God,
>   according to thy steadfast love;
> according to thy abundant mercy
>   blot out my transgressions.
> Wash me thoroughly from my iniquity,
>   and cleanse me from my sin! (vv. 1-2).

The consequences of David's sin remained. The child he and Bath-sheba had conceived died, but David received true forgiveness. Later he and Bathsheba had another child whom they named Solomon. Solomon was richly blessed by God.

The only healing response to such deep guilt is confession to God. Confession allows God to reestablish community with us. If we allow solitary time in which we search our hearts and confess to God, God will cleanse us of our sin (see 1 John 1:9). God will bring us into relationship with Him through Jesus Christ. We are then healed from such brokenness and given communion with God. Solitude with God leads to community.

The pain of death.—We also face powerful aloneness in the face of death. Certainly this is the most powerful of our alone times before God. We go to great lengths as individuals, families, and a society to cover the raw facts of dying. Most die in a hospital or nursing home, far from our vision. Funeral homes do us the service of making the deceased "look natural" and provide a safe place for grief to be expressed. But our death is ours alone. No matter how many persons love us or how much we are at home with self, our death is totally alone.

I have witnessed some faithful persons fight and struggle with death. Others die quietly. But each experience of death is a profound expression of being cut off. Cut off from self, loved ones, and life projects. Death is clear evidence that we are ultimately cut off from everyone and everything. Those who are brave enough to anticipate and contemplate this reality discover a special burden of aloneness. No quantity or quality of love, work, or play can take away this burden.

Aloneness and Solitude

If this aloneness is so central to human experience, is futility then the answer? Do we declare with the writer of Ecclesiastes, "All is vanity" (1:2)? This experience of loneliness cannot be met by under-standing self or by relating to others. This loneliness is neither emotional nor social. It is deeply spiritual. Spiritual loneliness is an inner striving for relationship with God. It is my heart's awareness of my need for God's presence and love. This loneliness can be met only by God. The primary human avenue to this awareness of God's presence is solitude.

Solitude is a difficult experience to describe. Solitude may be being alone but not necessarily. I may experience solitude in the midst of a huge crowd of people. This is the experience of "solitude of the heart."[1] Solitude is "a paradoxical state of being alone and yet not alone."[2] In solitude, I am alone in my inner self, yet I am very aware of the presence of God as well. My conviction is that the essence of the life of Christian faith is experienced in developing solitude with God at the center of life. I hope the meaning of solitude will become clearer as we go along.

How can we face our essential loneliness which we experience in our search for God? One man has written: "Religion is what the individual does with his own solitariness. . . . (R)eligion is solitariness; and if you are never solitary, you are never religious."[3] He was not writing about the revealed religion of Jesus Christ. But he was reflecting upon our human striving to cope with the facts of our existence, especially death. He was calling our attention to the many ways in which we attempt to cope with our awareness of finitude when the only true answer is found in our solitary relationship with God.

The Christian message is that Jesus Christ comes in the midst of these strivings to affirm that all things belong to God, and all is used toward God's purpose. Because of these facts and through the gracious love of Jesus, we are encouraged to risk loving. "There is no fear in love, but perfect love casts out fear. For fear has to do with punishment, and he who fears is not perfected in love. We love, because he first loved us" (1 John 4:18-19). Love of God is sometimes expressed in care of others' needs. Solitude offers quiet spaces where we can experience the love of God directly from God. Thus solitude is a pleasant and freeing experience of God's love.

The story of Billy Mills offers a contemporary statement of how separation from family and God is quenched only by knowing one's place as a child of God.[4] As Mills tells his life story, he was born one of twelve children to a Native American father and a French-Native American mother. He was accepted by neither the dominant white culture nor the Native American culture. His mother died during Billy's childhood, and then his father died when he was twelve. He truly had no family and no place. However, he started competitive running. He ran so much and so fast that he was the surprise winner of the gold medal in the ten-thousand-meter run at the 1964 Olympic Games. Now he was accepted. His Native American culture bestowed honors on him, and the white culture offered him a livelihood. He married, had children, and lived comfortably. But he still did not feel at home. He finally returned to his childhood home and consulted with the spiritual leader of his tribe. The leader heard his tale and then spoke truth: "The answer you seek lies with your Creator. . . . We are made to walk the spirit road with our Creator. When you walk the spirit road, you may journey through any country in peace." Billy knew the man was right and suddenly recalled the words of his father who had taken him to church and counseled him to begin each day with worship. He also knew that the words which his father had spoken to him were also the words of his Heavenly Father: "You are my son, and you belong. You belong to me." Billy Mills had learned the depth of God's presence and the need for solitude in which to allow God to enter his life.

Spiritual Conversion and Loneliness

This description of our human situation as one of ultimate aloneness may be quite disturbing to some readers. To reflect on this core of aloneness within our life experience raises many questions. For example, if the human spirit is finally thrown into this kind of ultimate aloneness, is there any genuine hope for human community? Another objection probably arises with the word *solitude*. How can solitude be healing for aloneness, especially the aloneness of guilt and death? Or, what hope is there for us?

Scripture clearly describes our brokenness, our separateness from God. Scripture also clearly describes the path we are to follow in accepting God's healing of our disease. *Conversion* is the word used to talk about the process of healing. Conversion offers the way God establishes within us "at-one-ness" in the midst of our ultimate aloneness, disconnectedness, and brokenness. "We love, because he first loved us" (1 John 4:19). We experience God's love in the depths of our aloneness. Christian conversion is ultimately an individual acceptance of God's love. Thus, conversion involves solitude. Solitude is a method of conversion. The Christian community is the context for conversion. But our knowledge of God's peace at the center of our being is ultimately met only in solitude.

The psalmist was well aware of both the pain of aloneness and the promise of solitude. During one deeply trying time he wrote these words: "My God, my God, why hast thou forsaken me? / Why art thou so far from helping me, from the words of my groaning?" (Ps. 22:1). Our deepest aloneness is frequently experienced as distance from God. Sometimes we even feel God to be entirely absent. Yet the psalmist also knew the healing of this aloneness. "Even though I walk through the valley of the shadow of death, / I fear no evil; / for thou art with me" (Ps. 23:4). The psalmist's deepest affirmation of God's presence was also expressed by: "My flesh and my heart may fail, / but God is the strength of my heart and portion for ever" (Ps. 73:26). Thus, our deep aloneness of God forsakenness is transformed into our deepest awareness of God's presence. How can this happen?

Conversion is the experience of God's graceful presence. The word *conversion* usually refers to persons initially committing their lives to Christ. However, conversion also describes the ongoing experiences which deepen our closeness to God. It is especially appropriate when we have been through a time of distance, of aloneness. The experience of conversion provides change and continuity at the same time. I am different, but I am still me. The difference is that I now know that God is with me and for me in all aspects of life.

The result of conversion is both inward peace and outward love. "The movement from loneliness to solitude can make it possible to convert slowly our fearful reactions into a loving response."[5] Conversion enables us to move from loneliness to compassion. Solitude is the route through which our ultimate loneliness becomes compassion. Our religious faith generates our sense of meaning and purpose because we are assured of God's presence. This assurance provides the deepest resources for dealing with our sense of loneliness. Two stories describe this transformation. One story is biblical; the other is from the religious imagination of an early English Baptist.

Joseph and Solitude

The biblical story of Joseph is one of intrigue, mystery, and the fulfillment of God's promises. It is also a story of loneliness converted through solitude by God's grace into compassion (Gen. 37; 39—47). I will tell his story from this vantage point.

Joseph was the favored son of Jacob. His favored status, however, separated him from his ten older brothers. I suspect Joseph experienced loneliness from both emotional pain and lack of community during his childhood and adolescence. He was isolated from his brothers and doted upon by his father. One day he took a message to his brothers who were away from home tending their father's flocks. Their anger toward Joseph was so great that they sold him to traders bound for Egypt. Imagine his isolation, sadness, and anger!

In Egypt, Joseph experienced injustice and imprisonment. These factors certainly cause feelings of aloneness and loneliness in most people. But his God-given wisdom was such that he was raised to political power. He was entrusted with the nation's food supplies during a severe famine. It was during this time that Joseph's brothers came to Egypt to purchase grain. He tested their loyalty to his father and other brother. Finally, after years of separation Joseph was reunited with his family! These are the facts. The depth of the human story requires only a little imagination.

Can you imagine the pain Joseph felt as he was so hated by his brothers? Imagine the ache of loneliness which fell upon Joseph as he was taken from his homeland to Egypt. He was betrayed by his own brothers, separated from his father, and lived with unfamiliar people who worshiped unknown gods. Joseph certainly experienced the pain of not belonging, the ache of missing family, and the emptiness of no community with whom to worship God. In spite of this pain Joseph prospered. He remained faithful to the dreams and visions of his youth. Although he lived among a strange people, he relied upon God's faithfulness. His aloneness was transformed into solitude with God. Thus, he was given wisdom and power. Joseph's wisdom was shown in that he did not use his power for personal gain. Rather, he cared for the people of Egypt with compassion. Later he had opportunity to take vengeance upon his brothers. Instead, he was reunited with his family and performed compassionate service to them.

Joseph was one who overcame loneliness by service. The pain of his aloneness was converted to the joy of compassion. Throughout the ages, Christians have expressed their compassion for others. To care for the lonely among the aged, the ill, and the homeless is an ancient Christian virtue. By Christ's example we are invited to wash feet and touch lepers. The only way we gain the courage to do this is through inner conversion. This conversion changes those who are lonely into servants as children of God. Like Joseph, we are called to develop times and places of solitude in order to be of service to others.

The Pilgrim's Progress and Solitude

The wonderful spiritual novel *The Pilgrim's Progress* by John Bunyan also offers deep insights into the nature of aloneness and solitude in the spiritual life. It illustrates the nature of spiritual conversion as a movement from aloneness through solitude to compassion. It is certainly no accident that this classic account of the Christian journey was written by a Baptist preacher while he was in prison. John Bunyan preached in England during the late seventeenth century. The first half of *The Pilgrim's Progress* was published in 1678 and the second half in 1684. Bunyan was imprisoned for preaching the gospel without an official church or government license. He was thus clearly aware of struggles in the Christian life. He was also clearly aware of aloneness as he was separated from his wife, children, and church for long periods of time.

The main characters in *The Pilgrim's Progress* were Christian and his wife Christiana. The first half of the book tells of Christian's spiritual journey from his conversion through many spiritual trials to reaching his heavenly peace with God. The second half of the book recounts the journey of Christiana. The book is an allegory. This form of literature tells a moral story through using individual persons, places, and events to stand for another—more general— meaning. Bunyan does not hide the meaning of his characters. He gives them names which are obvious to all who have experienced such people and events. Places such as Doubting Castle, Hill Difficulty, and Mount Calvary immediately remind us of such times in our own lives. People such as Faithful, Hopeful, and Worldly Wiseman are given faces out of our past. The universality of Bunyan's story is easily demonstrated since it is one of the best-selling books in history.

The story begins as Christian leaves his family to begin a journey to the Celestial City. His first companions, Obstinate and Pliable, leave the City of Destruction with him, but they fall away at the Slough of Despond. Bunyan is aware that companions on the spiritual journey may support or may discourage and mislead. His helpful companions include Faithful and Hopeful. Those who would distract him from his journey include Blind-man, No-good, High-mind, Liar, and Ignorance. Christian's journey takes him through many spiritually dangerous experiences. He calls these by many creative names; for example, Mount Sinai (the old law of sin and death), the Valley of the Shadow of Death (blasphemy and temptation), Vanity Fair (pride and flattery), and Doubting Castle (failure to trust God's promises). Eventually, Christian passes through the Delectable Mountains and the Vineyards and arrives home in the Celestial City.

Bunyan's central message is that neither reason nor knowledge are adequate guides for reaching the Celestial City. Rather, our personal experience of God turns us from aloneness to solitude with God. There is a stream of dangers and distractions along the journey. Doubt and despair are never far removed. It is a lonely hero's journey.

However, Bunyan also demonstrates that fellow travelers are essential in making the journey fruitful. He does this by telling us of both Christian and Christiana's spiritual journeys. The key difference between the two journeys is that Christian's is a solitary journey, with an occasional fellow traveler. Christiana's is never a solitary journey, but she has companions all along the way.

The Pilgrim's Progress creatively teaches us that the spiritual journey begins with a once-for-all conversion. But ongoing conversion is required as we grow in grace and seek to allow God to become an ever-stronger power in our lives. Christian faces many of his toughest tests while alone. The aloneness of his journey is emphasized. However, Christiana's journey is with companions. Bunyan knew the wisdom of balancing solitude and companionship. Both solitude and a committed community are essential on the Christian journey.

> The importance of community for spiritual growth is one of the most important single nuggets of wisdom that can be mined from the past. Writers like Bunyan remind us that spirituality is not something that we learn by ourselves, but something that arises as we take our place within an intimate and sustained community of saints.[6]

As we face our unavoidable loneliness before God, we remember the importance of both solitude and community. Bunyan's Christian and Christiana vividly teach us that both solitary time with God and supportive times with friends are essential if we are to allow God's love to enable us to face our depth of aloneness without despair.

The Promise of Solitude

The biblical story of Joseph and the fictional story of "Christian" are very different. Yet they point to the basic truth of the Christian's experience of spiritual loneliness. Our life journey is full of temptations which will deceive and distract us from companionship with God. The only effective and powerful answer to these temptations is times of solitude with God. Thus, solitude holds the promise of meeting our deepest loneliness. This is another paradox. Aloneness is necessary for loneliness to be healed. Solitude will not take away spiritual loneliness. It will allow us to directly confront our pain and allow it to be carried by Another.

Jesus' Experiences

The crucial importance of solitude in relationship to God can be clearly seen in Jesus' life. He repeatedly withdrew from the crowds and sometimes left His disciples in order to go to "a lonely place." (See Mark 1:35; 4:10; 6:31-35; 6:47; 7:24; and parallels, especially in Luke.) At times Jesus needed aloneness in order to pray. In prayer, He experienced the solitude in which His deep assurance of His oneness with God was nurtured. He needed aloneness in order to experience solitude with His Father.

But solitude was not the end of Jesus' spiritual journey. The Christian can never be satisfied with personal communion with God. Jesus' solitude was followed by increased ministry. For example, on one occasion Jesus' solitude was followed by His teaching a great crowd. When it was late, and He realized the crowd did not have provisions for a meal, He fed five thousand people from one boy's meal (Mark 6:30-44). His solitude led to powerful teaching and vigorous ministry to the people. Our lives should reflect no less commitment to both solitude and ministry. When these are combined, spiritual loneliness has little room to exist.

After feeding the multitude Jesus again sought solitude (Mark 6:45-52). During this time of solitude and communion with God, a storm blew across the lake where His disciples were in a boat. They were terribly frightened. Jesus then came across the water to His disciples with a message of comfort. In other passages we read of the same series of events: Jesus was alone, He prayed in solitude, people in need of ministry gathered, a miracle of compassion was offered. Solitude and compassion were repeatedly linked in Jesus' life.

In Luke 22:41 we read that Jesus withdrew from His disciples in order to pray. It was near the end of His earthly life. He was in the garden of Gethsemane. The clouds of political anger and religious rejection were fast rising around Him. He sought out solitude in order to once again confirm within His heart God's will. The noisy crowds of Jerusalem and the anxiety of His disciples were not conducive to hearing the voice of God. All these people added to Jesus' spiritual loneliness. He had to find a place of solitude in order to clearly hear God's will for His life. Here is another pattern of solitude: conflict, aloneness, solitude, and confirmation.

Perhaps the most powerful expression of this connection between aloneness and solitude is found in Jesus' words from the cross. In His most alone moment, Jesus was praying for God's presence (Mark 15:34; Matt. 27:46). Jesus probably quoted "My God, my God, why hast thou forsaken me?" from Psalm 22:1. This emotionally stirring psalm begins with the psalmist's expression of the pain of mortal illness, but it ends with a promise of praise to God.

> All the ends of the earth shall remember
>   and turn to the Lord;
> and all the families of the nations
>   shall worship before him.
> For dominion belongs to the Lord,
>   and he rules over the nations (vv. 27-28).

Even during Jesus' deepest time of aloneness He recalled a prayer of praise to God. Here the pattern of solitude is somewhat different: aloneness, solitude, fear of death, and promise of God's presence. Clearly, solitude was Jesus' way of confronting the fear of death. Solitude is an essential element as we seek to face this reality.

Jesus Christ knew the pain of aloneness. He transformed this aloneness into solitude and was empowered for compassionate service, facing conflict, and for going through the fear of death. Because of His experiences, there is little wonder that the hymn "Tell It to Jesus" is a favorite.

> Tell it to Jesus, tell it to Jesus,
> He is a friend that's well known;
> You've no other such a friend or brother,
> Tell it to Jesus alone.
>
> Are you weary, are you heavyhearted?
> Tell it to Jesus, Tell it to Jesus;
> Are you grieving over joys departed?
> Tell it to Jesus alone.

> Do the tears flow down your cheeks unbidden?
> Tell it to Jesus, Tell it to Jesus;
> Have you sins that to men's eyes are hidden?
> Tell it to Jesus alone.

Jesus clearly demonstrated that solitude transforms aloneness into compassion, confession, and courage. When we seek His presence in solitude, He is indeed a friend to whom we may turn. In Him we know the truth of solitude as the avenue to heal our spiritual loneliness.

How to Experience Solitude

Scripture is clear that times of solitude were crucial in the life of Jesus. How much more important must they be for our lives! However, those who feel lonely may find it very difficult to create periods of solitude. Modern life does not offer many opportunities for the quiet time essential for the development of solitude. Yet relationship with God demands this time. In what ways can those who suffer from spiritual loneliness create the space necessary for solitude to enrich life? The following paragraphs will suggest concrete actions which may create openness to God's presence. In God's presence we may experience the conversion of our aloneness through solitude.

Prayer.—The place to begin companionship with God is in prayer. This may appear to be a trivial suggestion. Indeed much that we call "prayer" is trivial. I want to discuss a form of prayer which is not trivial and which leads to the quenching of our spiritual aloneness. Much of what is discussed here can be found in Edward Thornton's book, *Being Transformed: An Inner Way of Spiritual Growth*. If what I write catches your attention, you will want to read his book for further guidance.

The first requirement of prayer is to set aside time for prayer. When? That is not important. It may be early in the morning, at lunch, or late at night. The time depends upon your particular routine, or lack of routine. Jesus met the demands of His intensely busy life by setting aside time for communion with His Heavenly Father. Can we expect to grow in relationship to God by doing less? The prophet Jeremiah also affirmed this basic first step. "I sat alone, because thy hand was upon me" (Jer. 15:17). When we wish to experience God's hands, aloneness is required. The space and time for such creative silence with God may occur in crowded places and busy days or in quiet places and open schedules. The openness of our hearts to God is all that is required for there to be time with God.

The second requirement is a proper attitude. Our attitude should focus on anticipating a conversation with God. Certainly this was Jesus' attitude as He sought aloneness in the Judean desert. Yet unlike conversations with friends, our conversations with God will usually begin in silence. The prayer which heals our spiritual aloneness is a prayer of the heart. This ancient form of prayer is grounded in Paul's statement that "the Spirit helps us in our weakness; for we do not know how to pray as we ought, but the Spirit himself intercedes for us with sighs too deep for words" (Rom. 8:26). Our attitude in prayer is an inner communion between the longings of our hearts and the Spirit of God.

The third requirement is that we use few, if any, words in prayer. This form of prayer is not word prayer. It is silence before God. It is prayer in which the sighing of our spirits is most directly expressed. Mental, emotional, and physical relaxation are often the beginning points of this prayer. But the essence of "prayer-of-the-heart" is a quiet being in God's presence. Thornton writes poetically about this profound prayer experience.

> The prayer-of-the-heart is not thinking about God. It is wholeheartedly longing for God. From time to time it is experiencing the Presence of God. Being lifted out of yourself by a powerful spiritual force is the way some people speak of the experience. Being bathed in love, joy,

and peace; enveloped in light, enlightened by truth, and awakened to your own true self—these are some of the images people use to try to tell what happens in prayer when the mind is in the heart.[7]

In this discipline of prayer we truly experience God as "Our Father," as one who lives in an intimate and loving relationship with us.

I can say no more about this prayer discipline here. Please refer to Thornton or to Henri Nouwen, *The Way of the Heart* for fuller treatments of silent prayer. However, I must emphasize that this prayer does not leave the one who prays alone with God. Rather, this experience allows God to take us into community shared by all persons. In this community love is birthed, experienced, and energized for human relationships. Solitary prayer never allows us to escape relationships. It always takes us back with deeper service and compassion. In this sense then prayer is a way to transform loneliness into solitude.

Meditation.—Meditation is another method through which our spiritual loneliness may be met through solitude. Whereas prayer focuses upon our relationship with God, meditation focuses upon our relationship to God's creation or to aspects of human creation. Whether our focus is on Creator or on creation, we are likely to find new depths of relatedness. Traditional philosophy has thought of finding the highest values for living in what is true, what is good, or what is beautiful. In fact, many intellectual and religious disagreements have developed when one person emphasized one value while another emphasized something else. Spiritual friendships are not deepened when one insists that morality (the good) is the most important spiritual value while another argues that intellectual clarity (the truth) is essential to spiritual maturity. Meditation seeks to examine truth, goodness, or beauty in such an appreciative way that life is deepened and solitude becomes companionship.[8]

Meditation upon truth in God's creation is recognized by Christians who study science. By studying biology, zoology, and other such disciplines they are convinced that they will have a fuller and more positive appreciation for truth. Meditation upon the truth in human creation is often the focus for philosophers and lawyers. Curiosity, patient exploration, and abundant questions are necessary for one who would meditate upon truth. A danger of this path is that the truth seeker can get so caught up in an intellectual process, that he or she can miss the companionship found in creative silence.

Meditation upon goodness in God's creation is characteristic of those who enjoy nature. Bird-watchers, gardeners, and campers may allow their times of quiet meditation upon the goodness of what they see, hear, and feel to deepen their sense of communion. Meditation upon the goodness in human creation may focus on acts of love and charity. The human virtues are valued as they are lived. Perhaps Francis of Assisi represents one who truly meditated upon the goodness of both God's creation and human creation. We see in Francis one who experienced his aloneness as times for wonder and awe in response to both God and fellow persons. Cheerfulness, generosity, and compassion are likely found among those who meditate upon beauty. A danger they face is that human evil or nature's dark power (earthquakes, tornadoes) may leave them disillusioned or open to manipulation.

Meditation upon the beauty of God's creation may focus upon the colors of the desert, the scent of a rose, the texture of a warm beach, or the call of the morning dove. Meditation upon the beauty of human creation may focus upon the colors of a painting, the smell of fresh-baked bread, the movement of a ballet, or the melody of a favorite song. Careful meditation may lead one to a deeper at-one-ness with the One who inspires creation and creativity. The danger of beauty is that the meditator may be deceived into substituting pleasure for beauty. While pleasure can be enjoyed, it should not divert the meditator from deeper communion with beauty. Those who meditate through beauty are strongly aware of their creative senses and unafraid of using these bodily responses in moving from loneliness to solitude.

Thus both God's creation and the inspired creations of humans offer powerful opportunities for companionship. To be nurtured by meditation requires that we enter a creative silence and appreciate what has been created. One who is willing to do so will find deep wells of companionship. Those who truly plum these depths will also meet the powerful presence of their Creator. Conversion, transformation, and new purpose will surely follow.

Spiritual companions.—A third way by which solitude transforms spiritual loneliness is through spiritual friendship. Spiritual friendship is somewhat different from any of the levels of friendship discussed in chapter 4 (convenience, intergenerational, and so forth). A spiritual friend is one with whom we can share prayer and discuss our relationship to God and God's creation. This level of friendship is very difficult to obtain. We are shy and anxious about discussing the deepest longings of our hearts for God's love, grace, and mercy. We are uncomfortable sitting in silence with others focusing together upon God's place in our lives.

The intimacy which develops in a spiritual friendship is different from the intimacy in other levels of friendship. Spiritual companions feel close to each other because they share an attachment to God through Jesus Christ.[9] Their attachment is not primarily enjoyment and comfort in each other. Their attachment is enjoyment of the presence of God and finding comfort in God's presence. Together they find encouragement, direction, and challenge in their spiritual journeys. Together they seek to allow the presence of the Holy Spirit to work in their lives, to develop obedience to God's directions for their lives, and to offer support during times of crucial life decisions when faithfulness to God is of utmost importance.

Ideally, spiritual companionship should emerge out of participation in the life and ministry of a church. I fear such relatedness actually seldom happens in most churches. We tend to be too busy doing good, building effective programs, and promoting special projects. Our busy-ness makes it difficult to set aside the silence, to go into a "desert" with a friend or two, to patiently wait upon the Lord. Certainly persons who are converted to Jesus Christ become part of "the people of God." The "people of God" and "the kingdom of God" are the central biblical metaphors for those who are following God's path (Judg. 20:2; 2 Sam. 14:13; Ps. 47:9; Heb. 4:9; 11:25; and 1 Pet. 2:10). Yet the "people of God" would do well to allow spiritual companionship to become a clearer aspect of their lives together. Spiritual emptiness and loneliness would not be so prevalent if solitude and prayer together were truly nurtured through church congregations.

Some may object that I have no grounds for the above sentiments. However, the available research does support my concern that persons in churches are just as lonely as those outside churches. It is true that persons who have a significant degree of personal religious commitment do report less loneliness than persons without religious commitment. However, persons who attend church regularly but express less personal, intrinsic value in their religious commitments are just as likely as nonchurchgoers to be lonely. In addition, participation in other social institutions (clubs, schools, and so forth) relieves loneliness just as well as participation in church. No measurable difference has been found in the loneliness of conservative believers, nonconservative believers, and nonbelievers.[10] Although this research directly measures emotional and social loneliness, I believe the results would be just as true of spiritual loneliness. Some people do not find their spiritual loneliness touched by participating in church activities.

Spiritual companionship can be nurtured through churches. Classes can be taught on prayer, meditation, solitude, and friendship. Out of these classes persons can be encouraged to identify two or three others who they would like to join in seeking God's presence together. They may need to meet occasionally with one who is more experienced in spiritual companionship for guidance and encouragement. The trust and privacy necessary for these groups to function can be threatening to the "fellowship" of the church at large. Thus, sometimes it is better for spiritual companions to find each other outside the congregations in which they worship.

Prayer, meditation, and spiritual friendship are powerful ways through which spiritual loneliness can be transformed by the presence of God. There are certainly other methods of increasing solitude which allow such transformation to occur. However, these three have been tested by Christians throughout the ages. They are well worth our investment today.

Conclusion

This chapter has explored the nature of spiritual loneliness and offered suggestions as to ways in which such loneliness can be transformed. The core method for such confrontation is to increase solitude. By increasing solitude the spiritually lonely person will paradoxically discover the abiding presence of God. Further, it should be clear that the discipline of solitude does open us to others. Jesus' commandment to "love one another as I have loved you" moves us from a simple affirmation of love for God to involvement with brothers and sisters on the spiritual journey.

Psalm 107 exudes the joy of this journey. This was a thanksgiving hymn sung by pilgrims on their way to Jerusalem for worship. They recounted the dangers through which they went to reach the Temple of God. Their praise was thus informed by intimate awareness of times of danger and aloneness.

> Some wandered in desert wastes,
>   finding no city to dwell in;
> hungry and thirsty,
>   their soul fainted within them.

> Then they cried to the Lord in their trouble,
>   and he delivered them from their distress;
> he led them by a straight way,
>   till they reached a city to dwell in.
> Let them thank the Lord for his steadfast love,
>   for his wonderful works to the sons of men!
> For he satisfies him who is thirsty,
>   and the hungry he fills with good things (vv. 4-9).

The physical dangers these pilgrims experienced were similar to the spiritual dangers faced by Christian and Christiana in Bunyan's novel. Like the experience of Christians today, they sometimes wondered whether they would be overcome by those dangers. Yet within a community of other pilgrims they praised God. They were preserved during their lonely struggles. They discovered their joy together as the people of God. This is the power of solitude to transform life and lead us into the joy of the people of God.

Jesus' disciples certainly experienced this transforming presence. After Jesus' crucifixion two disciples were sadly returning home to Emmaus (Luke 24:13-35). They were grieving. They were alone. Their spirits were broken because of the absence of their Friend and Teacher. A stranger slipped into their presence. He explained Scripture and offered them hope. Later as they broke bread together they recognized the stranger as Jesus. Even though He immediately disappeared, they were no longer alone and broken. They experienced a deep transformation in which their solitude was an occasion for overwhelming joy.

The pain of ultimate aloneness is resolved in the promise of solitude. Jesus' words ring clearly, "Lo, I am with you always" (Matt. 28:20). This is the deepest answer to our need for meaning in faith. Our need is for community with the God who challenges, promises, and reassures.[11] We are challenged in our aloneness, promised in our solitude, and reassured in our practice of compassion. Hence, our deepest loneliness waits on our acceptance of the presence of God at the center of our lives. Only here is our deepest loneliness ultimately relieved.

This loneliness finds its comfort in the creation of a deep center to life.

Life is meant to be lived from a Center, a divine Center. Each one of us can live such a life of amazing power and peace and serenity, of integration and confidence and simplified multiplicity, on one condition— that is, *if we really want to.*[12]

The person who creates opportunities for meditation on beauty, for silent prayer, and for compassionate friendship is allowing this divine center of life to grow. Solitude provides the space for this growth. Here we experience conversion from aloneness to wholeness.

Notes

1. Henri J. M. Nouwen, *Reaching Out* (Garden City, N.J.: Doubleday, 1975), p. 25.

2. Robert E. Neale, *Loneliness, Solitude, and Companionship* (Philadelphia: Westminster Press, 1984), p. 54.

3. Alfred North Whitehead, *Religion in the Making* (New York: Macmillan, 1926), p. 16.

4. Billy Mills, *Guideposts,* Feb. 1987, pp. 10-13.

5. Nouwen, *Reaching Out,* p. 34.

6. Brian Donst, "Communing with the Saints," *The Christian Ministry,* 17. Nov. 1986, p. 19.

7. Edward E. Thornton, *Being Transformed: An Inner Way of Spiritual Growth,* (Philadelphia: Westminster Press, 1984), pp. 65-66.

8. Benedict J. Groeschel, *Spiritual Passages: The Psychology of Spiritual Development* (New York: Crossroad Publishing Co., 1984), pp. 6-11.

9. Kenneth Leech, *Soul Friend* (New York: Harper and Row, 1977), p. ix.

10. Raymond Paloutizian and Craig Ellison, "Loneliness, Spiritual Well-Being and the Quality of Life," *Loneliness: A Sourcebook of Current Theory, Research, and Therapy* eds. Letitia Peplau and Daniel Perlman (New York: Wiley and Sons, 1982), pp. 224-237. See also Brian Dufton and Daniel Perlman, "Loneliness and Religios-

ity: In the World but Not of It," *Journal of Psychology and Theology,* 14 (1986), pp. 135-145.

11. Robert N. Bellah, et al, *Habits of the Heart: Individualism and Commitment in American Life* (Berkeley, Calif.: University of California Press, 1985), pp. 55-84.

12. Thomas R. Kelly, *A Testament of Devotion* (New York: Harper and Brothers, 1941), p. 116.

6

Caring for the Pain
and Claiming the Promise

You may have been reading this book in order to better understand your own loneliness. On the other hand, you may have been reading in order to understand better how to help a loved one who is lonely. You may be asking, "How can I care for those who are lonely? When I have a friend who is lonely, how can I respond?" Loneliness is clearly a painful experience. But loneliness clearly offers a promise as well. We have explored the pain and promise of loneliness through the life cycle and through three faces of loneliness. We have also discussed some ways that lonely persons can change or cope with loneliness. This chapter will focus on caring for others.

I find it somewhat difficult to suggest strategies for caring for those who are lonely. There are so many different faces to loneliness that it is difficult to suggest responses that will help. Even when a particular form of loneliness has been identified, there are great differences in how individuals respond. Nevertheless, it is important that family and friends who care about lonely persons have some guidance in how to care for the lonely. This chapter will offer such guidance based upon the biblical and human science understandings established in previous chapters.

Beginning Steps

There are a few basic steps which those who care for lonely persons should implement. Both laypersons and professionals can utilize these strategies in offering care. These include developing within yourself a proper attitude, developing relationship awareness, and identifying the form of loneliness.

A Caring Attitude

The starting place for offering care to the lonely is implied in my question, "How do I care for my lonely friend?" The question is *not,* "How do I take care of my friend?" The difference between "caring for" and "taking care of" may be subtle, but it is essential. My task with a lonely friend is to express my love, care, and concern to them. When I "care for," I open a loving space in which my friend can experience either relationship or solitude depending on the need.

"Taking care of" implies an over-under relationship in which I am superior, healthy, and whole. I cannot take care of another who is lonely. Such an attitude is more likely to leave my friend feeling even more lonely. The opposite of loneliness is a sense of another's interest and understanding. Thus, my first task is to create a loving space, not to take control of my friend's life. In this way I support his or her energy for the search which loneliness creates. The first and most important step is for you to offer yourself to your friend who is lonely.

Developing Relationship Awareness

A second step in caring for the lonely is to begin helping your friend develop awareness of relationships.[1] As one who cares for a lonely person, I too must develop my own relationship awareness. Fish live in water with no awareness of the water they live in. We live in air with no awareness of the air (unless it becomes polluted or scarce). Likewise, we tend to live in relationships with little awareness of how we are relating.

The lonely person needs to begin developing relationship awareness. Some adolescents may be mature enough for this step. They may be able to begin "seeing me as others see me." Some will not develop this capacity until adulthood. This step can be particularly painful if your friend has abused or been abused, has abandoned or been abandoned, or has not developed friendship networks even when they were available. Sometimes this added reflection on loneliness will leave your friend feeling even more lonely. Nevertheless, just as confession is essential if forgiveness is to be received, so awareness of relationships is essential if the promise of loneliness is to be claimed.

You can develop relationship awareness within yourself by several exercises. For example, you might benefit from listing your friends according to the categories suggested in chapter 4. These included convenience friends, special-interest friends, historical friends, crossroads friends, cross-generational friends, and close friends. Once you have listed your friends, you could develop further awareness by remembering ways each were special in your life and ways you have been special to them. For another exercise, you could ask a trusted friend, pastor, or counselor to help you see and feel more clearly the ways you relate to others. They are, of course, many other such exercises. The key point is that by enriching your own awareness you will be better able to help friends develop their own awareness of both present and potential relationships.

Identifying the Form of Loneliness

The third step in caring for the lonely is to help your friend locate the specific form of loneliness. Sometimes this step may include helping your friend name his or her pain as loneliness. Your friend may have been calling the pain headache, depression, boredom, or "nothing to do." Your friend may find it painful to clearly name the form of loneliness, but this is essential if the promise of growth is to be claimed.

Naming the loneliness may also include determining the length of time your friend has been lonely. Those who are chronically lonely have felt alone and without satisfying relationships for more than two years. Those who are situationally lonely have felt alone since a specific crisis (death, leaving home, divorce) separated them from relationships. Those who are transiently lonely experience occasional and brief moods of aloneness and separation. Friends who are chronically lonely suffer from profound emotional, social, and/or spiritual separation. They will have the most difficulty changing their lives. Situational loneliness is more open to change as the specific crisis is resolved. Transient loneliness implies little need for focused change but may call for patient openness to growth.

One question you may help your friend consider is: "How is your loneliness a season in your life journey?" For example, is your friend experiencing the season of loneliness that frequently occurs between young adulthood and middle adulthood? They may be experiencing vocational indecision, doubts about marriage, and deep questions of the meaningfulness of life. Or your friend might be going through the season of old age, adolescence, and so on. Although naming loneliness as being related to a life transition does not take away the loneliness, it can make the loneliness more bearable.

Other types of loneliness are more related to emotional emptiness or social deficits. Emotional loneliness tends to be rooted in early losses or low self-esteem. Social loneliness is more related to lack of satisfying relationships. You might help your friend identify a history of traumatic relationships or poor social skills. Another type of lonely pain could be based in her relationship to God. Your friend needs to realize the source of pain because the methods for claiming the promise of healing vary depending upon the source.

Other principles of care will need to be discussed according to the type of loneliness being experienced. Any suggestions will have to fit the context, condition, and intensity of the loneliness the person is experiencing. A key element in all these resolution strategies is to focus concretely on what your lonely friend can do now. Let us examine more closely methods of offering care to those in need of healing.

Caring for Loneliness During the Seasons of Life

Loneliness rooted in "my time in life" demands first that I accept the inevitable loneliness. The first step in caring for a friend who is lonely due to life transitions is to help them accept their loneliness as an experience which most persons encounter. Such acceptance will not take away the pain. Knowledge that others are going through similar pain will not take away pain. However, such acceptance will support your friend's process of living and of change. There is no quick resolution in this first step. There is much care.

There is a very fine line to walk in caring for the loneliness of life's seasons. Although such loneliness is "normal," it is none the less painful. Loneliness at any age should never be minimized, ignored, or given less than your full attention. For example, adolescents are frequently lonely. No amount of social, family, or spiritual nurture can totally protect an adolescent from loneliness. However, that does not mean that caring adults should not be concerned about their loneliness. Each friend needs to face loneliness as his or her own.

Children

Loneliness in your children is most likely when they are separated from one or both parents. Older children are most likely to experience loneliness when friendships have been disrupted.

What can you do when you are concerned for a young child who seems isolated from one or both parents? One strategy is to offer stability and adult love in another setting. For example, adequate day-care facilities in which student-teacher ratios are small enough for each child to receive individual attention are essential. Another strategy is to offer clear support and love to the single parent whose resources are likely extremely stretched. If she feels your love and care, she is more likely to have emotional energy to nurture her child. Support for a stressed parent and surrogate parenting sometimes pay no immediate dividends. They are future investments since we know that children who suffer emotional loss at an early age are more at risk for illnesses later in life. We hope that care now will prevent serious problems later.

Older children more often feel loneliness when separated from friends. The rapidly changing world of childhood insures that interests will change, different ability levels will emerge, and "bosom buddies" will drift apart. While these changes are normal and necessary, do not minimize the child's pain. Rejection and isolation at any age can be devastating. A sensitive parent or adult friend can care for the child by helping the child identify what changed in his or her relationship. Children do not automatically see that since Susan takes dance lessons three days a week and Jane plays softball three other days a week, their friendship will not be as close as when they played together every afternoon after school. Susan may still feel lonely. But she is likely to accept her loneliness when she sees some of the reasons for their separation.

It is particularly crucial that we help children avoid self-blame for changes in relationships. When relationship failures result from basically different interests, abilities, and uses of time, no one is to blame for the changes. Loneliness is inevitable. Of course, when a child has directly hurt another or has acted in unfriendly ways, they need to accept clear responsibility and attempt to restore the relationship. Usually children have natural ways of working out such hurts. I recall an incident from my childhood when a good friend and I got into a fight while playing basketball. A few days later my father noted that we were playing together again and inquired into what had happened. I responded, "Hey, Dad, you don't expect me to be mad at my best friend forever, do you?" Adults are much more likely to hold grudges than are children.

There is another way in which adults can care for the loneliness of children. In institutional settings (schools, churches, community groups) we need to give more reward for cooperation and helping. We tend to set up systems which are extremely competitive. Classrooms, sports, scout groups, and Sunday School classes are based on who can learn the most, who can win the most, and who can memorize the most. Some children can never be the smartest or the fastest. But all children can learn to cooperate and help others. Those who do so are less likely to be lonely. Adults can be alert to ways to reduce isolation and increase friendliness in any group of children for whom they are responsible.

Adolescents

Loneliness is unavoidable during adolescence. The other seasons of life have natural loneliness, but it can be avoided. Not so during adolescence. The emphasis of adolescence is on relationships, appearance, and on forging a personal identity. Each of these emphases carries a high risk of loneliness. Adults who sponsor teenagers through these difficult years offer a significant resource.

Adult sponsors for youth are crucial when the youth has poor relationships with parents. Of course, all parents have less capacity to be heard by their children during these years. Some parent-child relationships become totally ineffective. However, the mother of a friend, a coach, or another trusted adult can sometimes be heard very clearly. It may be a painful struggle for parents to allow their son or daughter to care more for other adults' advice and companionship than their own. Parents' willingness to take a backseat may be crucial to the development of the teenager's life direction. Adult sponsors play an essential role in this process. This first step in caring for the loneliness of a teenager is to be available as a trusted sponsor.

One way that sponsors enable development for teenagers is to help each identify the interests, skills, and potentials which are realistic for further development. Frequently the adolescent has difficulty testing what is realistic to hope and work for. If the youth can focus on areas of work, play, and love where success is possible, self-esteem is likely to be enhanced. When self-esteem is high, friendly relationships are more available.

The importance of groups should never be underestimated for adolescents. However, whether the teenager belongs to the in-group or the out-group or no group, loneliness is inevitable. Those who belong to the in-group will feel the loneliness of being responsible for holding that group's standards whether or not the standards fit that individual. The loneliness of the in-group can be cared for by encouraging more self-assertiveness and less responsibility for thinking, talking, and dressing like "everyone else."

Those who belong to the out-group will feel the loneliness of lack of status. Sometimes the out-group is held together by poor self-esteem and antisocial attitudes. The loneliness of members of the out-group can be cared for by enabling them to remain in contact with peers and adults who offer satisfying relationships, regardless of their status.

The loneliness of members of no group can be even more distressing. Youth who are ostracized because of lack of social skills and/or unattractive physical appearance are at great danger for severe loneliness. Adult sponsors will want to carefully support their social engagement in ways that their abilities and interests can meet. Sometimes these adolescents can be coached in both behavior and personal care that will allow better relationships to emerge.

Loneliness can be a great motivator for change among youth. Sensitive adult sponsors can support these changes and offer guidance toward more creative and satisfying relationships.

Adults

Both young adults and middle adults have a very reduced risk for loneliness. However, those who are lonely live in great pain.

The young adult who has difficulty forming intimate relationships is at risk. Likewise, the young adult who has been unable to identify meaningful work may suffer from significant loneliness. Each of these risks are usually visible to those who care for the young adult. Those who care can be of help during this season by offering companionship and support. It is crucial that the young adult come to a realistic perspective of his or her strengths and weaknesses in relationships. Thus, "relationship awareness" exercises can be very helpful. One reason for the difficulty in forming relationships can be abandonment or abuse suffered during childhood. When these experiences are present in lonely persons' history, professional counseling may be essential if they are to come to terms with their pain.

Middle adults have the least natural vulnerability to social loneliness. However, spiritual loneliness may be a great danger during this life period. Middle adults who are lonely have usually distorted the balance of work, play, and love which is necessary for healthy living. Friends of those who are lonely from unbalanced lives can support attempts to bring order and balance to life. This can be very difficult for the fifty-year-old-man who has grown accustomed to working sixty hours per week and not having any recreational activities.

The pain of having extreme commitments to college-age children, elderly parents, and leadership at work and church is also a source of loneliness. The loneliness of over-responsibility is sometimes met by letting go of what can be let go of. At other times letting go is not a realistic option. Then friends can only offer support during a difficult period of life.

Vulnerability to loneliness is also increased among those who have undergone the trauma of divorce, death of spouse, or multiple geographic moves. Informal connections with social groups can be very helpful following these experiences. Thus, support groups for the divorced and newcomer groups for those who have recently moved offer excellent resources. Other groups may be equally effective in dealing with loneliness. Sunday School classes, exercise classes, and volunteer activities may offer the emotional and social nurture needed. Friends who care can help the lonely discover these resources and support their involvement.

Elderly

Elderly persons are much less lonely than younger persons perceive them to be. Both married and unmarried persons report less loneliness than others would suppose. The key ingredient in a sense of community for the elderly is the development of an inner life of positive interests. Those who are content with their place in life and have inner resources on which to draw experience little loneliness. If you are a friend of an elderly person who is lonely, you may care by enabling them to identify their own resources. In this way they can develop a life-style which keeps them in touch with the future.

Sometimes elderly persons find relief from loneliness through nostalgia. They may remember people and incidents from their past and love to reminisce. Friends who can listen and enjoy this activity are invaluable. However, such nostalgia should not be simply a retreat into the past. It can be an opening into the present and future which energizes the older adult for creative living.

Friendship with a lonely older adult may involve enabling the person to identify those with whom they enjoy companionship. As with all ages, confidants are essential for feeling connected and appreciated. As the elderly exercise as much control as possible over their life, they are less likely to feel lonely. They may need help with transportation, financial resources, and staying in touch with compatible companions. However, as much personal control as they can have in these areas is crucial.

The lonely older adult who is healthy can be supported in activities which are of help to others. Volunteering time and energy in hospitals, community fund raising, church activities, and community social needs can frequently relieve loneliness. Through such activities they are likely to meet others with whom they can establish friendships. Those who are more physically restricted can be of support to others through letter writing and prayer. Letter writing offers a way to stay in touch with significant persons, no matter where they live or their level of mobility. Intercessory prayer establishes connectedness at deep levels of reality which generate companionship, even when presence is not possible.

Caring for the Emotionally Lonely

In chapter 3 I explored the emotions frequently associated with loneliness and ways to nurture growth in the presence of such emotions. There we stressed that those who are emotionally lonely can increase their self-esteem and grow emotionally through involvement with others and through solitary activities. How can those who care for the emotionally lonely help support this growth?

A very good place to begin is through helping the person identify activities and places they enjoy. Once they have identified enjoyable activities, you can enable them to increase the frequency in which they participate in them. This can be helpful even if the activities are solitary. Any enjoyable activity will improve your friend's morale and lessen their longing for friendships. Because loneliness is rooted in this longing for relationship, any reduction in the longing will decrease loneliness, even if the number and quality of relationships have not changed.

Your friend may need your help in order to increase enjoyable activities. She may need help with child care. She may need information on where to go to involve herself in a particular interest. Occasionally, she will need support in obtaining or budgeting financial resources, so an activity can be pursued. It is important that you enable

them to involve themselves in their own interests. Do not subtly co-
erce them into your activities.

Ventilation

A more powerful way of caring for your emotionally lonely friend
is to encourage him to freely and fully express his feelings of hurt,
anger, and despair. This expression is ventilation. To ventilate one's
loneliness is to talk about as much of the feelings and images of loneliness as one can be aware of. Some loneliness began in childhood
when your friend could not establish feelings of trust, acceptance,
and affirmation. Thus his pain is very deep. You may not feel competent to hear such deep pain. Or you may recognize that even though
your friend has shared deep pain with you, nothing seems to change.
He keeps expressing deep neediness. He does not seem able to make
any changes which offer promise of relief for his pain. In these situations counseling may be necessary for the desired changes to be
made.

Ventilation and catharsis (eliminating problems by talking about
them) may free your friend to move from loneliness to companionship. At other times he will stay stuck in old patterns of feeling and
behaving. As you care for his pain you will need to be prepared to
hear such expressions of loneliness without fear on your part. Your
calm and warm acceptance of his feelings and thoughts (no matter
how disturbing!) is crucial. At times you may cry with your friend
and otherwise deeply feel his pain. But you will take care that your
own experiences of loneliness do not add to your friend's burden.

At other times you will recognize that professional mental-health
help is essential for your friend to understand the roots of his emotional emptiness and to take corrective steps. In these situations you
will support his search for such help. Usually, your pastor will know
of such resources. Most communities have United Way agencies and
county mental-health treatment centers which offer competent help.

Certified pastoral counselors are also a valuable resource. You will not be able to push your friend into this kind of help. However, you can support his desires for health and wholeness as he takes steps to get the help he needs.

Modeling Companionship

Another way to care for your emotionally lonely friend is to be an effective companion. Such modeling will have several different aspects.

Since the emotionally lonely usually fear relationships, your friend will watch how you enter relationships. Are you able to control your own anxiety about starting new projects and meeting new people? How easily are you able to trust other persons? Your friend will certainly take note of your ways of initiating relationships. She may even copy some of your actions if you seem to be effective.

You may also care for your friend by practicing with her the feelings and situations she finds most difficult to face. For example, your friend may avoid relationships because she can never say no to whatever other people propose. The two of you could imagine various situations in which she would need to say no. Then she could find ways to say no in each situation with you attempting to persuade her otherwise. This exercise would build confidence and allow her to risk starting new relationships. Such practice can be very demanding but can also pay rich dividends for your friend. The purpose of this practice is to enable your friend to risk trust and relationship in spite of fears and anxieties.

Another area in which modeling can be effective is establishing realistic expectations for companions. The emotionally lonely frequently are so desperate for companionship that they set unrealistic expectations. For example, a lonely woman whose mother abandoned her as a child may consistently expect a mother's tender care from companions and fear they will abandon her as well. Neither expectation is realistic. Both are based on false assumptions due to her childhood experience. You may be able to call her attention to such distortions. A discussion of what she can realistically expect from others (including you) may free her for more effective companionship.

Realistic expectations also include that list of "shoulds" which most of us carry. We believe that people should act in certain ways. We believe that people should believe certain things. We believe that events should unfold in certain ways. These shoulds are frequently barriers for the emotionally lonely. You will care for your friend as you enable her to name her shoulds. She may choose to keep some and to discard others. Regardless, the shoulds will not block relationships as much nor prevent the intimacy which your friend so desperately wants.

A most difficult area in which the emotionally lonely frequently need good modeling is in self-imagery. Your friend may have a very distorted self-perception. She may perceive herself to be fat, when she actually is of average build. A man may see himself as a "jock," when he is actually quite ineffective at any sport other than television watching. A woman may believe herself to be dumb when she is actually quite bright and a very interesting conversation partner. She may not be able to remember any interesting life experiences when she has actually lived a very full (if sometimes painful) life. If your friend can improve her self-perceptions, she may not feel so lonely.

You can care for your friend by modeling accurate self-perception. The old wisdom of "Know thyself!" is crucial here. Then you can call attention to your friend's distortions. Be gentle and indirect when possible. None of us like seeing the ways in which reality is different than we suppose it to be. This is especially true when our self-understanding is negative and painful. It might seem that your friend would be ready to give up such pain. But I believe most of us prefer not to change, even when change would release us from deep pain.

Low self-esteem is especially powerful in blocking attempts to change. Thus, be patient and gentle, yet very clear, when you attempt to enable the emotionally lonely to face their distortions about self, others, and the world.

Friendship With the Depressed, Grieving, and Ill

Your friend may not be only lonely but also experiencing other emotional pain as well. Depression, grief, and physical illness are frequently accompanied by loneliness.

Depression.—Those who are clinically depressed need to consult with a mental-health professional immediately. You can recognize depression in family and friends by several signs. Have their eating habits changed substantially? Some people increase their eating while others almost stop eating when depressed. Have their sleep habits changed? They may have difficulty falling asleep, may experience sleep interruptions, or may want to sleep constantly. Do they seem fatigued with little energy for their usual pleasurable activities? Do they have feelings of worthlessness or inappropriate guilt? Do they have difficulty concentrating and become indecisive? Do they ruminate on death, express wishes to be dead, or have a suicide plan? If three or four of these characteristics fit your friend, he may be seriously depressed.

Your care for a depressed friend will be best expressed by supporting him as he seeks professional help. Many people will feel even less self-esteem because they seek such help. Assure your friend of your continued love and support. He is taking a courageous step in seeking help. You can affirm that step. Many times treatment for depression will also enable your friend not to feel so lonely. Your support can be a deep comfort at such times.

Grief.—Those who are grieving have varied needs for both companionship and aloneness. The loss of a loved one demands that we let go of our attachments to that person. Frequently, aloneness is important if those attachments are to be released. Thus, we can care for the grieving by allowing them time and space alone. But those who grieve must also reattach to new people and interests. Thus, we can also care by inviting them to stay involved in their circle of friends and to develop new skills and hopes.

This balance between providing space and offering presence is difficult to maintain. However, if you are sensitive to both needs within your friend and listen carefully to her expressions of need, you will be able to walk this delicate balance. Two cautions will help. First, grief takes much longer to resolve than we commonly expect. Intense grief is likely to be felt for three to six months. Ongoing grief may well remain for another six to eighteen months. Be patient with your friend and encourage her to be patient with herself. Second, the loneliness of grief cannot be avoided. It must be experienced if genuine healing is to occur.

Grief is not only related to people. We grieve when we lose possessions or have possessions destroyed. We grieve when we realize that a hope or dream will not come to fruition. We grieve when age or sickness takes away our physical capacities. These griefs can be just as profound as grief which follows death. Your friend will appreciate your patient presence and loving absence during these times as well.

Physical illness.—Physical illness is another occasion for loneliness. Your presence through visits, cards, letters, and phone calls will be of great encouragement. As your friend begins to heal, you can encourage her to reach out to others. Her reaching out will likely have some limitations. However, even those who experience ongoing disabilities can stay connected to their communities through prayer. They may also be able to stay connected through the telephone and letters. As you can support these connections, you will be expressing care for your lonely friend.

Support groups.—One method of care for those who are emotionally lonely is support groups. Support groups take many forms. Educational support groups focus on providing information necessary to effectively cope with the painful experience. One church offers an annual divorce recovery workshop over a four-week period. They provide the newly divorced with important facts and then follow-up with on-going small groups to provide companionship and care. A pastoral counseling center regularly offers community education events focused on various life crises. These seminars have enabled single parents, the grieving, and singles to better grasp their ongoing struggles.

Support groups for the ill are much needed. Hospitals are now discharging patients who are still in need of care and performing more outpatient surgeries. Many families then struggle to provide for the physical needs and emotional companionship of their loved ones. An invaluable resource is respite care for the sick. That is, trained persons may occasionally care for the sick person while the routine caretakers leave for recreation, shopping, and business needs. Support groups for the families of chronically ill and terminally ill patients also provide necessary support.

You may care for the lonely through these support groups. Your church might need encouragement to provide space and other support for one of these groups. You might volunteer your time as a respite caretaker on occasion. You could connect those who are lonely with the many support groups already available in most cities and many small towns. Such care will be of great significance to the emotionally lonely.

Caring for the Socially Lonely

The socially lonely suffer from a lack of relationships. This lack may be at many levels of companionship, but it usually focuses on insufficient "close friends." It may also focus on a lack of an "intimate friend." Social loneliness usually responds well to problem solving, skill development, and attitude-change strategies. Each of these approaches focuses on specific behaviors which must be employed if friendships are to be developed. The three approaches are certainly compatible. Indeed, all three may be useful for some persons.

One way you will care for your friend who suffers from social loneliness is to encourage him to explore one or more of the strategies suggested here. Your friend will undoubtedly have many objections to your encouragement. He may claim that he does not need such help. Be gentle but realistic in aiding your friend in an accurate evaluation of his strengths and weaknesses in relationships. He will almost certainly claim that he has neither the time nor money to attend the classes, to read the books, and to practice the changes. We have a great capacity for not wanting to change, even when we are presently in pain!

Although you may not have the necessary knowledge or skills to directly support your friend's growth in this area, a brief review of the various strategies will certainly help you appreciate your friend's needs. It may also help you to more accurately evaluate your own rational skills.

A Problem-Centered Approach

Some social loneliness is rooted in a person's failure to accurately evaluate her situation. A problem-centered approach to loneliness begins with a careful analysis of the source of loneliness. It then proceeds to develop step-by-step procedures for responding to the problems identified. How can you care for your friend who needs such change?

An assessment question.—A good first question for your friend would be: "With whom and with what and in what ways can I be a companion?"[2]

With whom? What kind of relationship does your friend desire? He will want to remember the different levels of relationship discussed in chapter 4. Is his loneliness most related to a lack of special-interest friends, to a desire for more close friends, or to a need for a special intimate friend? This question demands that your friend name his needs and goals for relationships.

With what? What does your friend have to offer to relationships? Is he knowledgeable in certain areas? Is he dependable and trustworthy? Is he a sensitive listener? Is he fun to share time with? This question demands that your friend count his assets and liabilities. This will allow him to determine realistic goals and necessary improvements.

In what ways? This question recognizes that social relationships come in many different forms. A balance of types and methods of relational attachments is essential. Some lonely people get into a cycle where they feel unloved and rejected while they act in ways which fail to attract other persons. For example, at work he may be constantly looking for a romantic relationship while missing the many opportunities for special-interest friendships. At church he may focus on recreation friends while missing opportunities to develop spiritual friendships. Others so desperately want relationships that they scare away potential friends with their heavy demands. Some are so fearful of intimacy that they sabotage opportunities to recruit persons to their interests. In what ways is your friend offering relationships?

Natural communities.—Another problem-solving strategy is to focus on the natural communities immediately available to your lonely friend. Natural communities are those relational systems which arise in the course of everyday life. They include groups such as churches, civic organizations, and family networks. Natural communities are contrasted with therapy groups, support groups, and other gatherings focusing on a particular personal need.

There are benefits for the socially lonely in being in communities, even when the levels of interaction and intimacy are low. These benefits may not be immediately evident to the emotionally and spiritually lonely. Therefore, as you can support and encourage your lonely friend to be involved in such natural groups, you will be doing her a great favor. Sometimes you may have to become involved in such groups yourself in order to encourage your friend's participation.

A Social-Skills Training Approach

Some social loneliness is rooted in a person's failure to develop the necessary skills for satisfying relationships. How can you care for a friend in need of better social skills?

You may care for your friend by encouraging him to enroll in various kinds of skill-development programs. These are frequently sponsored by the YMCA, YWCA, mental-health professionals, self-help groups, and some churches. Social skills training is appropriate for any age from childhood through elders.

Types of training.—Skill training focuses on needs such as how to begin relationships, asserting oneself appropriately, methods for conflict resolution, and appropriate self-disclosure. This training is effective both for those without relationships and for those with pained relationships such as broken marriages.

Skill training in beginning relationships will focus first on your friend's self-presentation. The first impression we make on others is indeed a lasting impression. Since many in our society judge much by physical appearance, your friend's ways of dressing, personal hygiene, and posture will go a long way in determining that first impression.

Also crucial to self-presentation is your friend's demeanor. Is his general approach to others open, warm, easygoing, quiet, hostile, withdrawn, happy, or scared? Demeanor goes below surface appearance and is more difficult to change. Indeed, most of us are not usually aware of how others experience our outward demeanor. Your friend might find your feedback helpful but threatening. For that matter, you might begin such a conversation by discussing your own demeanor. In this way you model the risk you expect your lonely friend to take!

Skill in beginning relationships is also dependent upon basic communication skills. The key aspect of communication skills is listening. Someone has suggested that God created us with one mouth and two ears, and we should use them in that proportion. If I can communicate to others that I understand their thoughts and feelings, then I will be a valued friend. There are many books and programs which do help improve these skills.

Another type of training focuses on self-assertiveness. Simply described, self-assertiveness skills enable lonely people to overcome shyness, take initiative, and express needs more clearly. Some have gained the mistaken belief that assertiveness focuses on expressions of anger and demanding what one wants. These are sometimes aspects of assertiveness but certainly not the focus.

Conflict resolution training takes communication skills a step beyond beginning a relationship. Conflict resolution focuses on how to proceed when ideas, values, needs, and/or feelings are different between people. Conflict may arise between persons in many different contexts. Those with inadequate conflict resolution skills may withdraw from relationships when differences emerge. Others may attempt to demand or force their own perspective, thereby leaving others angry and frustrated. In any case, the conflict tends to disrupt their relationships.

On the other hand, conflict and differences may enhance relationships if the persons involved have adequate skills. First, clear expression of one's own thoughts and feelings is essential. Second, one must also believe that no one has the absolute truth; rather, truth emerges in relationship. This attitude allows negotiation to occur in a win-win atmosphere rather than a win-lose or lose-lose situation. When all involved in a conflict can feel they have won, then conflict resolution has worked well. Finally, willingness to confront one's own inner feelings as well as other's expressed feelings is crucial. If I cannot bear the anxiety of being truthful in a loving manner about both my own and other's thoughts and feelings, then resolution is unlikely to occur.

This skill then bridges into the fourth major area of skill training. Self-disclosure is the skill of knowing how and what to reveal to others. Some persons develop anxiety if the conversation goes beyond "my name is," and, "Isn't the weather nice?" Others have a knack for spilling their entire life story, with an emphasis on the sordid parts, within five minutes of beginning a conversation. Neither style is likely to attract friends. Both will result in loneliness. Skill training for self-disclosure thus focuses on developing sensitivity to the level of a relationship and enabling the individual to express himself at that level.

Many youth, young adults, and "single-again" adults find self-disclosure training to be particularly helpful in dating. Dating roles are so dependent upon one's age and the nature of one's community that principles are difficult to generalize. An appropriate level of self-disclosure is essential in developing the intimacy to which most persons hope dating will eventually lead. Various workshops and books are able to help evaluate and change the lonely friend's level of self-disclosure. You can care by offering to practice such skills with your friend.

Skill-training procedures.—The procedures associated with each type of skill training have much in common. First, all emphasize practice of the skill desired. No matter how much I read about organ music, how much insight I have into the nature of the organ, and how much I imagine sitting at the keyboard and playing a Bach fugue, I will not play unless I practice. Indeed, I will not start by practicing a fugue. I will start with simple scales and simple tunes. When a lonely person has social skill deficits, they must start with the simple. They cannot enjoy the beauty of deep friendships or the joy of mutual intimacy until the simple first steps have been passed.

Most procedures first emphasize solitary evaluative activities. Through structured reflective exercises the lonely person is able to identify specifically what he needs to change. Another aspect of these activities is to allow the person to enjoy some solitary time. When the lonely person can enjoy solitude, much pressure is released which will enable them to more adequately relate to others.

The next level of training will involve group interaction and feedback. Casual relationships will be practiced. Clear feedback from trusted companions will be offered. Feedback allows the lonely participant to gain a clearer image of how others perceive her. This then can lead to more focused areas of change. As casual relationships develop within the training group, the lonely person gains confidence and hope in her ability to have friendships. Both confidence and hope are essential if initiative toward new relationships is to be undertaken.

Finally, skill-training groups provide support and feedback as the participants develop new levels of friendship and intimacy within the group. This generates even more confidence for engaging persons outside the safety of the training group. A basketball team can scrimmage with each other for weeks, but they never know their level of strength and competence until they enter a real game. The first game will give them incentive for much more focused practices. So skill-training groups usually offer follow-up support so problems encountered after training can be growth directed rather than growth blocking.

An Attitude-Change Approach

Some social loneliness is rooted in attitudes which your friend brings to relationships. When these attitudes are changed, more satisfying relationships frequently follow. Important attitudes to be developed include a willingness to take risks and patience with one's current relationships. You may be of help to your lonely friend in calling attention to both the positive and destructive attitudes which drive his behavior. In what ways can you care for a friend who needs to develop these attitudes?

An essential attitude for overcoming social loneliness is a willingness to take risks. Your lonely friend must first risk establishing an inner awareness of true thoughts and feelings. This is a courageous step since most of us tend to live with many illusions about self and others. Their true feelings may include self-doubt, fear of change, and self-hatred. They must also develop the willingness to take active steps to establish relationships. This may be difficult for both real and illusory reasons. The risk must be born.

A second essential attitude for the lonely person who wishes to change is to screen out the demand for "closeness" and "intimacy." The demand to "achieve love" may be almost overwhelming for singles in particular. This demand actually reduces the likelihood that a love relationship can be developed. It frustrates genuineness and trust which are the base elements in any significant relationship. The constructive attitude will focus on developing satisfying friendships. This "low-key" strategy will provide an arena in which trust can emerge. Thus, intimacy will have an opportunity to bloom.

Caring for the Spiritually Lonely

Spiritual loneliness is rooted in the reality of our aloneness before God. The essential process in meeting this loneliness is to allow God to enter the daily flow of our lives. The core step in allowing God to be present is solitude. One man has said this most clearly: "As soon as you are really alone, you are with God."[3] If this loneliness is rooted in solitude, then how can friends and family express care for one who is spiritually lonely? Are there any actions or words which can be helpful? How can I be a spiritual friend?

One person has suggested hospitality as the key image in responding to the lonely.[4] Since we are all strangers to each other, hospitality recognizes the importance of receiving any who feel they do not fit. Hospitality involves receiving, entertaining, and offering kindness. These can provide key themes for appreciating the nature of spiritual friendship.

Receiving friends and God.—Spiritual friendship begins with your attitudes and practices of receiving guests. There are certainly many approaches to being a host or hostess. As a spiritual friend you will be challenged to be host to your friend as the two of you make space for God. Quiet, respect, and reverence will form the center of your role as host.

How do you allow God to be part of the ongoing flow of your life? If you are to express care for your friend who is feeling separated from God, you will first have created a quiet place for God in your own life. Thus, you will have experienced awareness of your separation from God, allowed God to enter your life, and acquired practices which maintain your awareness of God's love and grace for you. My point is that in order to care for your spiritually lonely friend, you will have your own inner spiritual resources to draw from.

Entertaining.—Spiritual friendship also involves the role of entertaining. However, this role needs to be carefully considered. The central aspect of spiritual entertaining is making space for self, friend, and God. This role demands authenticity, honesty, and patience. The spiritually lonely may have great difficulty being patient with silence. They may have great difficulty allowing God to be present in God's own way. As host, you will "entertain" by encouraging, supporting, and modeling such patience and honesty.

Perhaps the core spiritual attitude you will need in your role as entertainer is a ready acceptance of loneliness as a fact of life. This means that you will not be panicked when your friend expresses feelings of spiritual dryness, failed prayer, and separation from God. You will know that these are part of our human experience and ways that God works within us. If you have this acceptance, you will be willing to enter your friend's loneliness. Rather than pushing for change and for immediate results, you will be able to patiently wait with your friend. This means you will protect your friend's solitude while offering your love. A good image of this is the way in which Job's friends came to comfort him during his time of grief. They came and sat with him without speaking. Any words spoken will enhance your friend's solitude. Your words should not distract from the spiritual struggle which forms the core of your friend's inner relatedness to God.

Offering kindness.—The spiritual friend will also offer great kindness. Out of your own deep experience of God's graciousness for you, you will offer the same kindness to your friend. Most of us live in such conflicted, demanding, painful worlds that any expression of kindness is like cool water for a parched throat. Such will be your gift to your friend.

The attitude of imagination will be crucial in offering such kindness. If we are to care for our spiritually lonely friends we will do so with imagination. You will exercise that God-given faculty which allows you to see possibilities that are not immediately present. Imagination allows you to know the inner pain of your friend and see possibilities for change. Imagination allows you to see how programs of evangelism, Bible study, and mission activities can personally apply to you and to your friend. Sometimes programs are done without concern for personal needs. Indeed, they are frequently ways to avoid confronting the fact of our aloneness. When used with care and imagination, they may be bridges to the deep sources of spiritual companionship.

A Delicate Balance—Companionship and Solitude

Our care for the spiritually lonely involves a delicate balance. Our lonely friends need to know of our love, care, and concern. But they also need to know of our respect for their aloneness before God. Thus there is a delicate balance between protecting their opportunities for aloneness and creating opportunities for community.

I am convinced that we cannot create spiritual growth in those we love. But we can provide opportunities for them to experience God's presence. We do this first by example, as discussed above. We also provide opportunities by being a spiritual friend. This step involves intercessory prayer. It also involves encouraging our friends to pray, especially contemplative prayer.

The goal of such spiritual friendship is the goal of the Christian journey—to love God and to love one's neighbor. Therefore, compassion for others is also a key. Our spiritually lonely friend will have a difficult journey. He or she is already well aware of aloneness. Spiritual disciplines will allow them to become aware of God's presence through their aloneness. The final step will carry our friend toward others. "We love, because he first loved us" (1 John 4:19). Their relationships will be marked by compassion, a deep care for what God intends for others.

As friends we can support the spiritual processes which lead through aloneness to compassion. We cannot force the completion of this journey. Often we will never see our friend's resolution. Our own faith is tested at such times because we long to see our friend's pain healed. However, as we live by faith, we are able to trust in that which is not yet seen by sight. We trust that out of our ultimate separation, God will bring a community of love and peace.

The ultimate answer to spiritual loneliness is strange. Spiritual loneliness requires aloneness. But this aloneness is with God.

Where to from Here?

The pain of loneliness is deep. The promise of change is ever present. The key to caring for a lonely person is to care. We must avoid the temptation to *take care of*. This principle was my first guideline. It is my last as well. The key is to care, whatever your friend's form of loneliness. It may seem somewhat simplistic to say that we care for the lonely by caring. But as we offer the grace of undeserved love to those who feel emotionally empty, socially abandoned, and spiritually deprived, we soon discover the great complexity of such care. We also discover the great joy of offering such love.

For Further Information

Some may be interested in learning more about loneliness. There are actually very limited resources available. I believe the resources listed here are trustworthy and interesting.

For those interested in other books written at a basic level of understanding, I would recommend two books. Samuel Natale, *Loneliness and Spiritual Growth,* offers a balanced understanding of loneliness. Although the book is focused for religious educators, many others who want to care for the lonely will find help here. Robert Neale's *Loneliness, Solitude, and Companionship* provides a good balance between therapeutic and spiritual emphases. Although it is not written from an evangelical perspective, there is much wisdom here.

Extremely useful resources are available from Guideposts Associates (Carmel, N.Y. 10512). They offer a videotape, "Loneliness: The Way Out," which is designed for use with small discussion groups. It covers many aspects of loneliness in a very helpful way. The video comes with a Leader's Guide and Discussion Guides. Guideposts also has available a pamphlet, "How to Overcome Loneliness," that some lonely persons may find comforting and helpful.

For those who are interested in more technical or professional information, there are three important books which provide an overview of the subject. Each is an edited collection of articles by a number of different authors. Robert S. Weiss, *Loneliness: The Experience of Emotional and Social Isolation,* was one of the first to bring together key theories, research, and interventions related to loneliness. His main contribution was in distinguishing between emotional and social loneliness. Joseph Hartog, J. R. Audy, and Y. A. Cohen, *The Anatomy of Loneliness,* collected thirty-one essays from a variety of disciplines including theology. Letitia Peplau and Daniel Perlman's *Loneliness: A Sourcebook of Current Theory, Research, and Therapy* is an excellent summary of a social-psychological perspective. It also contains an extensive bibliography.

A Benediction

Go now into the world of the lonely. Protect their opportunities for solitude and for community. Be with them in their pain. Offer hope that they can change. Enable them to change situations that can be changed. Do not despair that loneliness cannot be totally abolished. Rather face loneliness with courage and creativity. And know that the love of God, the grace of our Lord Jesus Christ, and the fellowship of the Holy Spirit is with you, now and forever. Amen.

Notes

1. Robert Neale, "Loneliness: Depression, Grief, and Alienation," *Clinical Handbook of Pastoral Counseling,* eds. Robert Wicks, R. Parsons, and D. Capps (New York: Paulist Press, 1985), p. 478.

2. Robert Neale, *Loneliness, Solitude, and Companionship* (Philadelphia: Westminster Press, 1984), p. 104.

3. Thomas Merton, *Thoughts in Solitude* (New York: Farrar, Strauss, and Giroux, 1976), p. 113, quoted by Neale, *Loneliness,* p. 479.

4. Neale, *Loneliness,* p. 123.